TWO WOMEN

TWO WOMEN

Harry Mulisch

Translated from the Dutch by Els Early

JOHN CALDER · LONDON
RIVERRUN · NEW YORK

This translation first published in Great Britain 1980
by John Calder (Publishers) Ltd.,
18 Brewer Street, London W1R 4AS
and by Riverrun Press Inc.,
175 Fifth Avenue, New York City 10010
Originally published in Dutch as *Twee Vrouwen* 1975
by De Bezige Bij, Amsterdam
Copyright © Harry Mulisch 1975
Copyright © this translation Els Early 1980

British Library Cataloguing in Publication Data
Mulisch, Harry
    Two Women. — (Riverrun writers; no. 5).
    I. Title
    839.3'T'36F   PT5860. M85T9   79-41752

ISBN 0 7145 3810 8 casebound

The publishers are grateful to the *Foundation for the Promotion of the Translation of Dutch Literary Works* for assistance in the translation of this novel.

Typeset by Visual Art Productions Limited, London W1.
Printed by M & A Thomson Litho Ltd., East Kilbride
Bound by Hunter & Foulis Ltd., Edinburgh

. . . Eros drenches the climate of my heart
as the wind roars through the oak forests on the mountain

SAPPHO

A few things have happened to me — not only the death of my mother.

The day before yesterday I was sitting in my workroom until deep in the night drinking a bottle of wine; suddenly a tiredness covered me as a dropped parachutist is covered by his parachute. From one moment to the next I couldn't focus any longer, and left everything the way it was, turning off the light, and going downstairs to lock the front door. In the letterbox was a telephone message to call Nice. I immediately understood what it meant. The nursing home had chosen this way to inform me in stages. First I would have a suspicion, then I would be well prepared when I heard the news on the telephone. Without even locking the door I went upstairs and called. Although it was nearly four o'clock I got through right away. Yes, she was dead. The afternoon before, the head-nurse said (her voice travelling with lightning speed through France, Belgium, Netherlands), she had fallen asleep in the park and had not woken up again. In the course of the evening her heart stopped. She had not suffered.

How did she know that? What she meant was that she herself had not suffered. I was instantly wide awake and sober. I knew that park, the Jardin du Roi Albert I, fifty yards from the sea. The surf is no longer audible and there is a filtered silence which is filled every afternoon by old ladies and gentlemen from all parts of the world. They sit endlessly, in the shade of the trees, by the rushing of the fountains, spread over the grass and the paths, slumped down in the municipality's wrought iron chairs or in canvas folding ones, sometimes beside a bench with a nurse reading a book, already far too much attracted toward the earth.

Some are already lying back in reclining chairs, with a rug over their knees, their hands folded. Amongst them walk mothers with children, whom they don't see any more; they are looking up into the clear, transparent green of the sycamores; seeing in the trembling leaves scenes which will disappear with them from the world forever. All the memories enacted in that foliage! Scenes in mansions, in sunrooms, at masked balls, on a honeymoon in Baden-Baden!

Under this roof of images she had fallen asleep for good. I said that I would take the first plane in the morning, then put down the receiver and looked outside. A year ago she had gone to Nice to enable this to happen. Three months ago I had seen her for the last time. We had parted without saying goodbye. What had happened then must have been the beginning of her death, which only now came as a confirmation.

The rain streaked through the light of the lanterns into the black canal, the cobblestones looking wetter than usual when it rains. Did I now have to go to bed and lie there just like my mother? I noticed that I was already calculating. If I got into my car right away I could be there by the next evening. My mother was lying on her back COLD with her marble face as white as her hair which was probably undone and spread out over the pillow as when someone falls, making her look like an old young girl. Her white hands indissolubly folded on the white sheet. Or she may be already somewhere in a dark cellar, a sheet from her toes to the tip of her nose, with a grumbling fan because it was a hot August night.

I pulled the small suitcase from the closet in my bedroom and started to pack. She had said once that she wanted to be buried in the South of France, near the Provence which was the setting of the famous book her husband had written in which love is invented once again, and which she had probably never read. She knew of a cemetery in St. Tropez which looked out over the sea — that should be arranged now or at least one should try to arrange it, because it might not be possible. I gathered up my cheque book, car papers and passport and took my raincoat from the coat rack. In the entrance way I now locked the front door from the outside. I thought: if there should be a little animal in the lock, a young ant, fled from the shower, it is now smashed up by the mechanism.

By the deserted canal my burning eyes looked briefly up at the rain. Further on in the city, where bars and nightclubs were closing, there was tooting and shouting. I felt something of the excitement of the journey I was so unexpectedly going to make. Even the inside of the car seemed to receive me with some astonishment, at this hour.

Once when I was ten, I ran away from home. Not because something unpleasant had happened, or because I was depressed, but because I suddenly wanted to go away; perhaps there was a special fragrance in the air, or a white cumulus on the horizon. I got my bicycle from the shed and rode through the city, in the direction of the sun, determined never to come back. I rode through villages whose names I knew but where I had never been. It was summer, that is to say, a summer of youth, therefore a warm summer, and an unending warm day. I biked hour after hour, while the space around my body became ever larger, as when I put on one of my mother's dresses. Away, I wanted, away. But when would I finally get there? Yes, I think that I actually thought that you could arrive at 'away', that it was a place, just like the house I lived in. It couldn't be much further now, away. I had biked half the afternoon, and the street under my front tyre became liquid like a grey river of stone. But the villages kept on coming, there was always another one on the horizon. Finally I grew faint and dizzy from hunger and thirst, but I had no money with me. I had thought that somehow this would be arranged when I got there. In a village I stopped near a vegetable cart and waited till the greengrocer turned his back on me while he was talking with a woman. Quickly I pulled a carrot from a bunch. Maybe the woman saw it, in any case the greengrocer grabbed my handlebars right away.

'Stealing?' he shouted. 'Are you allowed to steal? What's your name?'

'Henny,' I said.

'Henny who?'

'Henny Hoenderdos, sir.'

'Where do you live?'

'All the way back in Leiden.'

'Fancy that! You better get home fast or I'll tell your mother.'

The carrot was pulled from my hand and returned to the cart. I gave up. Who knows how far away might still be away. I turned around and went back the same way. The day was still bright, and hunger and fatigue now stretched every minute to an hour. I believe I became hypnotized. The stone cataract under my front tyre gradually upended itself and I had to bike up it vertically. When I came close to Leiden it was as if I were standing still and I **had to get the** whole earth rolling under me with my pedals.

At home the table wasn't even set for the evening meal. In succession I devoured four apples from the fruitbowl, core and all.

'Where have you been,' called my mother from the other room.

'At a friend's.'

'Who?'

'Henny Hoenderdos.'

She hadn't even noticed that I had been away; forever too. Since then no matter how far I've been from home, it has never been as far away as it felt then. Apparently I had not really understood that the earth is round: that that AWAY where I wanted to go could if necessary be my parents' house. But as a matter of course I had started to ride south; it never occurred to me to go north, direction Haarlem. North, south: I'm always vaguely aware of those two directions. When I lose them I sometimes figure it out with my watch the way my father taught me. The small hand must be aimed at the sun, the dividing line of the angle which the minute hand makes with the 12, points south.

'Do you understand?' My father smiled, on the veranda, steadily looking at me as if he wanted to imprint the concept

in me with his blue eyes. 'At twelve o'clock the minute hand
points south, but you must also take into account that the
clock-face is a whole circle, while the sun travels half.'

Already with his troubadours now. Mortz es lo rays. Somewhere up there, in Les Baux, on that slightly sloping plain
which looks out over Provence, roaming among the ruins
which are part of Richalieu's poetry.

I believe that I do a better job going from my kitchen to
my living room than from the living room to the kitchen; not
because it is the kitchen — I don't mind the kitchen — but
because it's north. On holidays I always know where the
most southern point of my journey is. In Nice, visiting my
mother, I always swim extra far out on the last day until I
haven't touched bottom for a long time, and then I think: this
is the most southern point, from here on starts the trip back.

That the sun goes from left to right when I face it is the
same thing. Of course I always forget that left is called east
and right west, until I remember 'the sun rises in the East.'
I've sometimes asked people who have been over the equator
if they didn't find it strange that the sun there moves from
right to left, counter clockwise. But never did anyone say,
'Yes, of course.' It seems that nobody has ever noticed it,
while I, if abducted under sedation to the southern
hemisphere, would know within half an hour from the
movement of the sun that I was there. Some people think
that I mean that below the equator the sun rises in the west
and sets in the east. How extraordinary that so few people
have a sense for that kind of thing. For me, the movement of
the sun from left to right, in a southerly direction, is
implanted in my body as the metal cross in a casting-mould.

Henny Hoenderdos was in my class in grade four. Why did I pick him when the greengrocer asked my name when I came to the end of my flight? It wasn't because I didn't like him; actually I didn't like him, but that's not why I used his name. I said his name as a matter of course, as if it was my own.

Three weeks ago I met him again for the first time. I sat on the steps of the monument on the Dam, between some hundred boys and girls who were scarcely older than I was in the days of my flight. Only they had persisted. They had come from all directions to be part of this fantastic, colourful group in the middle of Amsterdam. They were sitting or lying around the white column which in actuality was a localized AWAY. There were soft sounds of guitars strumming and flutes playing, and I didn't belong there at all of course. I must have looked quite ridiculous, probably older than the policemen who were keeping an eye on them from a blue police wagon in a sidestreet. I sat amongst them that afternoon because I no longer knew how to go forward or backward in my life. In the middle ages there was a superstition that a man could cure his syphylis by sleeping with a virgin, – in the same way by being amongst these young people I thought to absorb some of their strength and freedom. The sun shone on their paradise-like island, surrounded by the whirling traffic with its stench and fury, and it was as if my problems gradually became more impersonal. The feeling which I harboured for someone had flapped loose in the wind, like a torn sail; that afternoon, on this windless atoll, it almost seemed to have finally come down so that I could get hold of it.

The middle-aged man who had been observing me for a

while from the steps on the other side, crossed over and
headed straight for me. He wore an old fashioned kind of
wind jacket above dark brown pants which were obviously
part of a suit; it was clear that he was not always dressed like
this.

'Well, is it you or isn't it?' he asked and looked down on
me. That pale, reddish hair!

'Henny Hoenderdos,' I said, but I didn't get up. Nodding I
looked up. He didn't smile, and I didn't either.

We had line-drawing class and Mr. Verheul was busy
putting a strange figure on the black board: a large circle or
ball, with a vertical cylinder emerging. Henny Hoenderdos,
on the other side of the aisle, had a smirk on his face as he
looked at me. I leaned over to him and whispered: 'It looks
like Verheul's prick.'

Right away he raised his hand.

'Sir.'

'Yes, Hoenderdos?'

'She said something funny.'

'What is it?'

'I can't tell you.'

'Then you had better whisper it in my ear.'

Henny walked to the front and started to talk behind his
hand into Verheul's ear. Verheul was looking at me and I saw
his eyes change. He got up and opened the door.

'Come into the hall please.'

He closed the door behind me, crossed his arms and looked
at me silently, which somehow made me uncomfortably
aware of his member in his wide Dutch pants.

'Did you really say that?'

'Yes sir.'

'Do you know what that means?'

What a silly question. Of course I know about a prick, even
if I don't have one. Suddenly I had the feeling that Henny
had told him something completely different, but I didn't
dare to ask.

'Yes sir.'

'Then you better go to Mr. Donker.'

Between the coats in the deserted hall I walked to the sixth grade where the principal was teaching.

'Yes, what is it?' he asked, absent-mindedly.

'I said something funny to Mr. Verheul,' I said, while the bigger boys and girls snickered.

'To Miss Borst,' said Donker without looking up.

Miss Borst taught second grade; I had to go up the yellow painted stairs.

'What do you want?'

'Mr. Donker said to come and see you.'

While the little kids giggled Borst held up her strapping hand and slowly beckoned with her fat index finger. I stepped onto the wooden platform, closed my eyes tight and at the same time got a hard slap on the side of my head.

'And get out of here. Don't let it happen again.'

She didn't even know what had happened. As an executioner I guess it didn't concern her.

Satisfied, his hands in his pants pockets, Henny looked at my red cheek when I got back to class.

'Henny...' he said. 'I haven't heard that for a long time.'

'Is it Henk nowadays?'

He didn't go into it.

'Are you in the habit of sitting here?' he asked.

'Yes, is that allowed?'

'With all these dope addicts.'

'Are you with the police these days, Henny?' I motioned with my head towards the police wagon.

He looked around, making a tense motion with his neck as if his collar was too tight; but the top button was undone.

'And you?' he asked.

'What do you mean?'

'What do you do?'

'I'm a curator in a museum, and you?'

'Something like that.'

He was still the same, still closed and underhanded.

'You're still holding down turkeys these days?' I asked. With raised eyebrows he looked at me. I said no more. If he wanted to be closed, I could be too. With satisfaction I saw that I had caused him some confusion. He looked at his watch. 'Yes, of course, you are busy,' I said. 'Don't let me keep you.' For a few seconds he looked at me, then nodded and left without a word. I watched him as he crossed, and crossed again, and finally disappeared in the distance beside the palace – probably forever out of my life.

The encounter didn't sit right with me, I suddenly felt ill at ease. Where was he sending me this time?

Once my mother had put the water on for tea, but a little later my father said that he'd really rather have coffee. 'Alright,' said my mother, who poured the boiling water into the sink and put on fresh water. I laughed so hard that I rolled on the floor, but my father said that he could see a strong distinction between water for tea and water for coffee.

'It could be that the coffee would have a bit of tea flavour.'

I tried to think of my mother, but I didn't think of her really. I could deal with her death, I mean, I was in a way glad that I suddenly had something which occupied my mind and caused me to leave the country and which allowed me less time to think of something else. When it started to get light I was already across the border. I had left the eightlane funslides near Antwerp behind me (wet and empty on Sunday) and approaching Ghent, I was driving between the first hills. Where the hills begin there Holland stops, and the work of men, the control takes over: there the world begins, the one we are all given. At that point, where morality changes to nature, I always sense a seriousness in me which I don't feel in Holland. It rises up in me as the earth rises up around me, it comes from deeper, harder, more elementary layers, — which in Amsterdam are covered over by a hundred meters of mud.

Those building pits in Amsterdam! Shuddering pumps to keep the ground water down between the dripping iron walls; workmen down below wading up to their knees in mud; concrete posts to support the building, otherwise it sinks into the muck, each year another story, until finally sopping and bubbling Holland would close itself above the roof. When our civilization passes no tourists will be able to admire our proud ruins. Amsterdam will disappear like children's sand-castles on the beach when the tide comes in.

Under the window of the room where I am now writing is also a building pit. Dozens of men wearing only shoes, short pants, and yellow hard hats, break a hole in the rock with pneumatic drills, now a hundred yards long, fifty wide, and twenty deep. It runs right to the bottom of the house; there isn't even six feet left in front of the door. Earlier it must have been a square. Roaring bulldozers scoop up the rubble like tyrannossauruses and dump it from their jaws into lorries which drive it away slowly through clouds of yellow dust. I think it is limestone. In that roaring ravine the sun shines.

Fortunately the written word is something which is audible without having to be heard. Even the most modest word which I write down, like the word SILENCE for example, speaks louder than the inferno in that pit of stone.

SILENCE.

'Remember,' I said, perhaps ten minutes after I had first spoken to her, 'I'm not a person who talks a lot.'

'I'm not either,' she said.

What was the matter with me? It was the kind of explanation someone offers in a café at the train station when one poor soul meets another who has responded to his marriage advertisement, and from the start the intent to stay together is obvious! Apparently she too felt this was no ordinary encounter. – For myself, I had already noticed it just looking at her from behind.

I had bought a loaf of bread. It was Saturday afternoon. There was a watery February sun over the city. I saw her on the other side of the street in front of a jeweller's window. I stopped. I looked at her back, her head, her calves which stuck out above bright red boots, and at the same time I wondered why I was standing there, looking. It was as if everything in the street had become vague and distorted, as in some pictures, while only that girl in the center remained clear. Not that she was so beautiful from the back. Her hair looked great, put up loosely, but her back was little too long, her hips too narrow, and her legs not as straight as is generally desired. Yet everything differed from the ideal in a way which somehow or other fitted exactly with ME. One's body is made up of expressions. Everybody agrees about the eyes and the mouth, and the hands, – but also the feet and the neck and the calves speak a language which does not lie. Cut off the head and the arms, it's still an ideal image which belongs in the Louvre.

I crossed the street. Suddenly I seemed to be panting. Never before had I felt so clearly from one moment to the next that I was doing something that was going to change my life. Never before had I been involved with a woman, and at that point I hardly realized what I was about to do. presumably I still thought I was being carried along by some sort of platonic, aesthetic feeling, as found in books.

'Would you admire those stones even if they weren't expensive and rare?'

I had joined her. My heart pounded. Surprised and scared she looked at me. At the same moment the traces of fear and anxiety disappeared from her face and I could see what she looked like.

I afterwards imagined that her face was exactly as I had expected it to be — so that, after seeing her from behind, I could have carefully reconstructed her face according to the methods the police use. Each person has a special curve which appears everywhere in his body and which is the expression of what he is. My mother had a faint S-shaped line in her upper eyelids, which appeared in the corners of her mouth and which also determined the profile of her neck and her hips, and she worked it into her hairstyle as well. In her case, standing beside her, there was a pointed ellipse, flat at the top, which I can only remember seeing in an Egyptian hieroglyph; this figure was apparent in her calves but also in her mouth and eyes, and even in the small boat-pattern on her T-shirt. Her face reminded me of Giotto, and of some frescoes from Siena by Ambriogio Lorenzetti. Her hands were bony like a boy's, the nails bitten short: I immediately decided to put an end to that.

'I never thought about them being expensive.'

It was the kind of shop which only needs one customer a day. The window display was predominantly beige. On linden green velvet a handful of unpriced objects were displayed. She pointed at a small, roughly-wrought golden owl with emerald wings, the head inlaid with diamonds and with two

topaz eyes. It was almost too beautiful to look at. Now that
everything is past, I can see that bird more clearly before me
than I can see her face, of which I only see half, — the other
having become invisible, as in a mirror.

'Would you like to walk a bit?' I asked.

'Okay.'

I felt like someone who has ordered lobster in a restaurant
but doesn't know how to eat it. In silence we walked beside
each other; for some reason I felt handicapped by the bread
under my arm. It was as if it indicated a completely different
direction than the one I was taking now, — namely to a weekend in which I would mainly sleep and perhaps read. No
longer could I imagine that it would happen that way, that
she would say after a while, 'Well, I have to go now,' and that
I would finish the rest of my shopping.

'Do you live in Amsterdam?' I asked.

'Wish I did.'

'Then where?'

'In Petten;' she said it with a hard p, as in spot.

'What's your name?'

'Sylvia.'

She patiently answered all my questions, but she herself
asked nothing.

'Do you have a job?'

'I work in a beauty salon in Egmond.'

'And your father? What does he do for a living?'

Apparently it seemed natural to get that information too.

'Superintendent with the Dyke Conservation Board.'

'That's neat,' I said.

'Yes, very neat.'

'Isn't it?'

'YOU try living there.'

The daughter of the superintendent of the Hondsbosse Sea
Wall, — three dykes in a row: the Watcher, the Sleeper, the
Dreamer, which kept the tumult outside in its place, and in
the antiquated insides of the Dreamer they had installed a

nuclear reactor, which was supposed to stop the tumult from within. Petten suddenly seemed like Holland's navel, the only place which could have given birth to her.

It was cold. We walked aimlessly through the streets, side by side. It still wasn't clear to me what I really wanted, only that I wanted to keep on walking beside her, like a dog beside his master; that is, a seeing-eye dog, because the boss took no initiative at all.

'Where shall we go?' I asked.

'You decide.'

'Do you have to do something special today?'

'Not me. I took a day off.'

Did I have anything special to do? I had been married for seven years and was now already divorced for five. I did my work at the museum, and the visits to my mother were also my holidays. Now and then I went to bed with a man I had met here or there. Usually this happened at my house. I wasn't interested in a permanent relationship; in any case, the man who wanted that usually had a family, and on the weekend ('you realize, darling, I can't think of anything I'd rather do . . .') they were usually tied up. I went to concerts of modern music, art exhibits, and sometimes to the theatre. Occasionally I would visit people, but gradually that happened less often. Twice a week I ate downtown, and on Sunday I didn't even get dressed. Yet I had never worried what to do with the rest of my life. I was about half-way now, but later? Getting finally to my pension as a grey, single, lonely lady held no terror for me, because it simply did not exist. I had always been sure that something would suddenly happen, on a certain day, − but only if I didn't look for it. Whenever you focus your will and attention on something it becomes invisible, unattainable, at least that is my experience. You really only see things from the corner of your eye, when you are actually doing something else. It's as if reality feels ignored, objects and then manifests itself.

'Shall we go and have a drink at my house.' I asked.

'Alright.'

'You have nice things,' she said as she sat on the sofa and rolled a cigarette.

'That happens when you get older.'

But she didn't ask how old I was. I opened the beer, poured two glasses and sat across from her.

'You want to roll one?' she asked and held out her tobacco pouch.

'I haven't done that for a long time.' I pulled out a paper and put some tobacco on it. My hand shook and she noticed.

'Are you in the habit of picking up girls on the street?' she asked.

'You won't believe this,' I said without looking up, 'but you are the first girl I ever picked up.'

'Are you married or something?'

She seemed detached but she wasn't. If anyone was being seduced it was me. To top it off the tobacco fell off the paper onto the floor.

'That was quite a while ago,' I said while I picked it up. I didn't care what she thought, I was caught and it didn't bother me in the least.

'Have you never been to bed with a girl?'

'No.'

'Sans blague?'

I smiled.

'Sans blague,' I said, 'and you?'

'Oh sure.'

'And with a man?'

'That too.'

'Doesn't it matter if it's a man or a woman?'

'As long as they're nice.'

That was really very spiritual and noble, if you thought about it.

'Was that a French boyfriend or a French girlfriend that you had?'

'Boyfriend. Shall we lie in bed for a while?'

I put the paper with the wad of tobacco on the table. I became totally disoriented, as in a dark but warm and moist and jasmine-scented forest. Without looking at her I got up and closed the curtains, mumbling:

'Nel mezzo del cammin di nostra vita
Mi ritrovai per una selva oscura.'

In a state of total confusion I undressed myself. I thought I was going to wet my pants from excitement. When I came out of the bathroom she was kneeling naked on the bed; in the dark red light which came through the curtains she looked at me with her thumb in her mouth. She was slender as a hieroglyph, while behind the curtains and all around the walls the city lay in winter.

'Shouldn't you put on a record?' she asked.

A record. This was hardly the time for Xenakis or Monteverdi. Satie perhaps? The Gymnopedie? Luckily I found something by Peggy Lee. I went to her and it was as if I had stepped over a threshold, broken through to something new. It had to do with that FRAGRANCE which I some-times, once a year, would smell — but also not smell, or imagine I smelled, which reminds me of a fragrance I must have smelled once, in primeval times. A whiff, in an alley, or on the staircase of a small hotel in some country or other, in Venice; but right now it was gone and not traceable, not even if I take a few steps back. A dark, warm smell of fresh bread and old blood which opens up to a totally different, forgotten world.

'You're nice and skinny.' she said.

We separated ourselves from the room and from the day and capsulized ourselves as an amoeba in the endless sea. I've kept no memories, it lies there in my life, in February, half a year ago — a blind spot, the place where the nerves leave the eye.

Afterwards we lay there for a little longer. She was so soft I couldn't feel where she began. She lay on her side and beside her I leaned my head on my hand while with the top of my middlefinger I slowly approached the flesh on her buttocks, they looked like a boy's, but when I saw that I had already pushed them in a little I still could not feel anything.

'Do you know that I seldom take a day off?' she said. 'Just like I knew.' She sat up. 'Shall I do something with your hair? It's full of dead ends. Do you have a decent pair of scissors? Most people have rotten scissors.'

With the shower hose, on the edge of the tub, she washed my hair. A little later I sat on a chair with a towel over my shoulders while she silently busied herself with me. I said nothing either. Both of us were still naked. When she turned off the hairdryer and said 'Finished, madam.' I asked:

'Will you come and live with me, Sylvia?'

'If that's what you want.'

'Yes.'

'Good.'

We got dressed and walked out into a washed, reborn city: master and servant — she the master, I the servant. I never did get past the one brown loaf in my attempt to buy groceries for the weekend, and I suggested we go and have some fondue bourginonne. This was apparently something new for her. The streets, the restaurant, the waiters, the tables, the people, everything was filled with well-being. That was not because of the world, it was because of her, because of us. Only very young children experience the world this way and perhaps, they experience it without the help of others, because they themselves are love.

While sitting across from each other waiting for the oil to boil in the blackened pot we discussed how the situation in Petten should be approached.

'They must not know **anything** about it.' said Sylvia, 'My father would have me hauled away by the police.'

'You have decided to get a place in Amsterdam. Today you found a room at my house. I'm your landlady.'

'And if he asks how I pay for that?'

'Then you have found a job with a top-notch hairstylist. In the Beethovenstraat. Or in the Hilton Hotel.'

'And I managed all that in one day?'

'On the contrary. You've been working on this for months, but you didn't want to say anything until you were sure. That was a question of honour for you.'

'Do you know what my father would do?'

'No.'

'He would laugh. He knows very well that I'm not like that. No, I know what. First I won't say anything for a week or ten days. That's happened before. Then I go back home and tell them I've met a student who I'm going to live with.'

'And if they ask about the student?'

She spiked a piece of meat with her fork and held it up, laughing.

'Then it is your son.'

Sizzling, her meat disappeared into the oil. I had no reply and put some meat in too.

'What shall we name my son, Sylvia?'

The same moment I realized that she hadn't asked my name yet — that would only happen the next morning over breakfast.

'Thomas,' she said seriously, as if she had already thought about it for a long time.

'It must be done now,' I said.

She took the meat from the boiling oil, but instead of putting it on her plate and then picking it up with another fork to dip it into the cool sauce, she put it directly into her mouth. I saw her lips stick to the fork and immediately discolour. But not a sound came from her mouth, her face remained unchanged, her eyes looking straight at me.

When, ten days later, she went to Petten to tell her parents of her engagement to Thomas, her lip had healed again. That night she came home with a big suitcase full of clothes and things.

'How did it go?'

'Alright of course.'

She considered it too unimportant for further discussion. Her parents had ceased to be in her thoughts from the moment she closed the door behind her. She put a doll on the bed and hung her clothes in the closet which hadn't been used for the past five years. A couple of old shirts were still there and she immediately put one on.

The first weeks we stayed home most of the time. Having each other was enough, and moreover I didn't quite know yet how I should act if we met someone. Though I didn't have anything to hide, I nevertheless found it exciting that my new life had so far been hidden from the world. In the morning I brought her breakfast in bed, by the time I went to the museum she had usually gone back to sleep. At eleven o'clock I phoned to wake her up, and when I came home at noon the whole house smelled of coffee and the table was set with fresh buns. In the afternoon she went out, shopping or to see a movie, or she stayed home and made clothes, or lay on the floor reading a book. She loved the modern Dutch literature, probably because, with the exception of a few authors, it is made up solely of a type of book designed for sophisticated young people which nobody reads after 25. In the evening we cooked dinner together, and afterwards we read or watched television. It amused her to make love while

the priest or minister on the 'close of the day' programme
looked at us with melancholy understanding. She also
augmented the neglected pop music section in my record
collection. After a while she only bit the nails of her right
hand, while those on the left became long and pointed.

'Let's go somewhere,' she said suddenly on a Sunday
afternoon.

'Then we'll take pictures of each other.'

I enjoyed that kind of impulse, and we took my camera
and went to the zoo. It was March and still cold, but already
it was quite busy.

'Each of us can choose an animal to pose with!'

That seemed like a good idea.

'I want to be over there,' said I, 'near the birds.'

'Why the birds particularly?'

'Because they predict the future.'

She took a picture of me with some kind of creature with
a red beak and a white comb.

'You too?' I asked.

She shook her head.

'I don't want to know the future. I'll see it when it comes.'

'Then with an owl. Remember, our golden owl? Owls are
wise, they predict the past.'

'Yes, with an owl!'

But we couldn't find one in the bird house, nor anywhere
else. While we were looking, she took pictures of me with the
deer and the zebras and the red ibis, but she herself could
not find an animal that she wanted to be photographed with.

'Not even with the puma?'

'He is beautiful,' she said. 'See how he walks.' He walked
as if he weighed nothing, as if the earth was not hard and
resistant. 'But still I don't want him in the picture with me.'

'Then maybe with a sparrow?'

'Let's go and have a look there, in the aquarium.'

But it turned out to be closed.

'Perhaps with him,' she said and pointed to a concrete

sculpture of a tyrannosaurus which stood opposite the entrance on the lawn.

She walked over and stood in an angular pose which she had copied from fashion models, and I took her with the fish-eye lens.

'I'm getting cold,' I said. 'Let's go to the reptile house.'

'Yes, here! here!' she shouted as soon as we had walked into the moist, tropical atmosphere. 'How many pictures do you have left?'

'Six'

I took four pictures of her with the crocodiles, the snakes, the iguanas, and the lizards, and I didn't have to worry that they would move and get out of focus. It was as if their endless past had given them the petrification of history itself — they sat motionless as if they would exist eternally.

'And now the two of us together,' said Sylvia. She took the camera from my hands and went to a boy her own age who was just passing.

'Hey, would you take our picture?'

She showed him where the shutter was, put her arm through mine and looked laughingly into the lens. When it was finished, she went to him, took the camera, and then put her arm through his.

'And now us,' she said and handed the camera to me.

I had to laugh, for now, after all the reptiles, now came the most extraordinary of all — a man. I took the picture and by way of thanks she gave him a kiss on the cheek.

After a while we started to go out together. Mostly to concerts, sometimes to a cabaret or a movie. Most people knew about us now. Old acquaintances no longer came by, and I did not seek them out. I did not miss them. I was satisfied with Sylvia, and as far as the men were concerned — apart from those who didn't care and who reacted to us in a normal way, I saw two different reactions in their eyes: lecherousness about those two women, or, more often, hatred, fury, because they were denied by us, destroyed.

'Zinnicq Bergmann Museum.'

'Good afternoon, this is Boeken. May I speak with Mrs. . .'

'Speaking.'

'Oh sorry, I didn't recognize your voice. '

'You don't hear it that often any more.'

'How are things with you?'

'Excellent, and with you?'

'Alright, alright, a little busy. We haven't seen each other in a long time.'

'Why should we?'

'How is your mother?'

'Not very well, she's getting old.'

'You still visit her?'

'Twice a year, as always.'

'Next time say hello for me.'

'I'll do that.'

'Tell her I still often think of her, and her husband.'

'How thoughtful, Alfred. Was that why you phoned?'

'No. You know very well why I called.'

'Then say so, love.'

'I've heard that you've become lesbian.'

'So?'

'Then it isn't true?'

'If you've heard that these days I live with a girl, that is correct.'

'That's what I've heard, yes.'

'People do talk. There are thousands of girls and women who live together.'

'Is it an ordinary friend?'

'Ordinary, ordinary. . .What do you mean by ordinary?'

'Did you rent a room?'

'Oh no, it is completely free. She even gets money to boot.'

'Well, well. Since when has this performance been going on?'

'You can only think in terms of performances. It is no performance whatsoever. It is a very special girl and I've known her for a month or two. Why should you care?'

'How old is she?'

'Would it excite you if I said sixteen? Or would you prefer twenty-six?'

'It doesn't excite me in the least.'

'I'm not so sure of that, Alfred.'

'You act so strangely. I thought perhaps she would excite you.'

'You are right about that. She is twenty.'

'If you ask me, there's something strange about this affair. You are not a lesbian in the least.'

'Then don't use that word.'

'Why do you live with a woman if you're not a lesbian? Is it perhaps the age? I recall. . .'

'Yes, if you insist, I recall that too. The night you came home like an idiot with some trollop or other, and you were interested in seeing us do it together. With you, I suppose, sitting in an arm chair with a cigar in your mouth watching the events. That turned you on even then.'

'Indeed. But you took your pillow and went to sleep on the sofa.'

'Right, and you sent that drunken tart out onto the street.'

'What?'

'Never mind.'

'So you're not a lesbian?'

'Then why do you keep saying that I am?'

'Because you live with a girl, dammit! What kind of a game is this anyhow?'

'Well, you figure it out, and be happy with your wife and your two children.'

'It isn't exactly a compliment in my direction.'

'So that's what it is. Do they look at you with a strange gleam in their eyes when they say that I've become a lesbian? If you ask me they think that after you I can't stand men.'

'Must you be so snide?'

'Never mind, you can tell them that after you apparently no man could measure up. You can give them any explanation you like. Explanations are your specialty; you even made it your profession.'

'I learned that from your father I guess.'

'Sure, blame my father.'

'Is it perhaps because you can't have children?'

For a moment I could not say anything. When I was able to speak again, I thought better of it and hung up.

In an exotic little shop we bought turkish rings which consisted of four separate, braided parts. They were held together by a thread which was not to be removed until the ring was on the finger. At home Sylvia took hers off to have a closer look and right away it fell apart into a chain of four links. She puzzled for half an hour how to put it back together again. Then the bell rang. Sylvia opened the door.

'Hey, mother!' I heard her calling. While her mother came up the stairs I walked quickly into the hall and saw Sylvia hurriedly taking her ring off again. 'Get inside and close the door,' she hissed at me with a look of authority which I had not seen in her before.

I did what she said and stayed behind the door.

'I was in town anyway,' I heard her mother saying, 'I thought I'd drop in for a minute.'

'Yes, that's alright,' said Sylvia, 'but he isn't here.'

'Thomas isn't home?'

'And we can't go to our room either, because it's an awful mess.'

'That doesn't matter, dear. How are you?' There was a moment of silence: obviously for a kiss. 'I brought three pastries. Do you suppose you could make some tea?'

'Mother, they're busy wallpapering and whitewashing, everything is pushed to the side and under dropsheets.' It came out so smoothly she must have prepared for this eventuality. 'But perhaps we could sit down in the landlady's living-room for a minute.'

'You mean Thomas' mother?'

I moved swiftly to the sofa and sat down. Someone knocked.

'Yes?' I said. I was sorry I didn't have some needlework in my hands.

Sylvia stuck her head around the door.

'Mrs. Boeken? I'd like you to meet my mother. Our rooms are. . .'

'Of course, Sylvia, of course, come in. For some reason or other she had used Alfred's name, which I never did any more, — now I think that she possibly did that on purpose so that her mother could not find me in the telephone book.

Her mother couldn't be much older than I, but it was obvious she had lived a different life. With a shopping-bag in her left hand she shook my hand, pumping it up and down and said:

'I'm Mrs. Nithart, pleased to meet you.'

'Nice to meet you Mrs. Nithart. May I take your coat?'

'Is this the day you have to attend the opening?' Sylvia asked me.

'I'll only stay a minute,' said Mrs. Nithart. She sat down in an armchair but did not lean back.

I took the box of pastries to the kitchen to make tea. The situation did not please me in the least. I felt you shouldn't deceive someone this way. While I waited for the water to boil I sat down at the kitchen table and considered whether I could walk in with the tea and say, 'Mrs. Nithart, I do not have a son and I never will have a son. I myself am Thomas. I love your daughter and she loves me. We sleep together and we are very happy. I don't know how you feel about these things. Many people still find it disgusting and unnatural. But nature itself is unnatural, as no doubt you know from the life of animals, especially if you have a dog where you live in Petten, which is quite likely in a superintendent's family, probably a German shepherd. And if only man could be natural. But he heats water for tea and he eats pastries without being hungry, and probably you will not find it as offensive if it concerns your own daughter. Mrs. Nithart, I ask you for your daughter's hand because we are planning to stay together.

Only I couldn't foresee the consequences. That thing about the police taking her away was of course nonsense: she was older than sixteen and she didn't live here against her will. But how would Sylvia react? What did I know about her relationship with her parents? She had never told me anything about them. Perhaps she would suddenly be overcome with shame and would no longer want to see them or me, and when she made a decision, she stuck to it. That much I had learned about her. I didn't dare. Besides I did take some strange sort of pleasure in the role I found myself in. I almost felt as if she really was my daughter-in-law.

With the tea on a tray, each pastry neatly on individual plates with small forks, I went into the living-room again.

'You know, Mrs. Boeken,' said Mrs. Nithart, 'we're so glad my husband and I, that Sylvia has finally settled down. Till now she was always. . .'

'Mother, for heaven's sake!'

'Let your mother finish, Sylvia. I like hearing more about you.'

'She has always been like that, you see. Nobody's supposed to talk about her. Even as a child she minded.'

'How modest.'

'Maybe, it's hard to say.'

'Do you know what time Thomas will be home?' Sylvia asked me.

'It would be nice if mother could meet him.'

'It might be late,' I said, while I hoped that my bafflement did not show in my eyes, 'in any case after dinner. There is another meeting of the students. Problems with a professor,' I explained to Mrs. Nithart. 'He seems unwilling to lecture until something or other is straightened out. I don't follow it exactly, perhaps you have read something about it in the paper. Thomas is against him, as far as I know.'

' I thought actually that he was in favour of him,' said Sylvia.

'Alright, in favour of him. In any case he studies less, whether he is for or against him.'

'What does he study?' Mrs. Nithart folded her hands in her lap and leaned slightly forward.

'Andragology,' I said, while I had the feeling I was going too far. 'Yes, I realize, you are not the only one that doesn't understand what that is. According to me nobody knows.'

'As long as Thomas knows,' said Sylvia with an injured look.

'Does it have a future?'

'That question applies I believe to the whole world,' said I as I stuck my fork into Thomas' pastry. 'But if need be he can always earn a living as a mechanic.'

Gradually I too became caught up in the craziness of it all, and Sylvia immediately responded: 'He has a motorbike, an old Harley Davidson. We often go out for rides.'

'Why don't you come down to Petten then on the motorbike? Your dad would like it too.'

'You know how it is, Mrs. Nithart,' I said. 'Although we live in the same house, I hardly ever see my son. These children insist on leading their own lives, and that's how it should be. It's only the housing shortage, or else they would have moved out long ago.'

'Are you happy with Thomas, Sylvia?' asked Mrs. Nithart in a way which indicated to me that this conversation should be ended immediately.

'Of course. Or else I wouldn't stay with him.'

I glanced at my watch so that Mrs. Nithart could see it.

'Yes, I have to go too.' she said and got up. 'I don't want father to come home to an empty house after work.' She hesitated a moment, and then asked me: 'Do you have a picture of Thomas perhaps?'

I froze. A mother without a picture of her son.

'Of course,' I said, except that, right now. . .with those painters in the house. . .'

'Never mind, just leave it.'

'But how about that picture at the zoo?' said Sylvia with astonishment. 'You took that one yourself.'

I didn't know right away what she meant — and when I suddenly caught on I felt like someone who's been sound asleep in the night when suddenly the bright light is turned on. From the envelope with pictures I looked for the one of her with the young man who had photographed us in the reptile house.

'What a handsome boy,' said Mrs. Nithart with the picture in her hand. She looked at me. 'He looks like you.' I nodded.

'But he has the eyes of my divorced husband.'

'Do you see those pants?' asked Sylvia. 'I took those in.' She took the picture and pressed her lips on it.

'May I keep it.' Mrs. Nithart asked hesitantly. 'Then we'll frame it and put it on the mantle piece.'

'But of course,' I said.

We said goodbye and Sylvia saw her mother to the door. Exhausted I fell on the sofa. When she came back into the room with a smile on her face I asked: 'Sylvia, tell me honestly, when you had your picture taken beside that boy, did you intend to use that in case you needed to show a picture?'

'Of course, what do you think? That's why I wanted to go and take pictures in the first place.'

She took her ring out of her pocket and started to put it back together again.

At seven-thirty I was at the French border. The sun was shining a little and I stopped at a roadside restaurant to buy Esso, change money, and get some food. There were already a few Dutch and Scandinavian travellers who had been driving all night. Babies screaming in their mothers' arms, toddlers clutching milk in a glass with two hands. Standing up I drank coffee with milk and ate a ham sandwich. It occurred to me that I had not thought of my mother who all this time had been lying on her back and would never move again. It bothered me that I didn't know how her body was lying in relation to me — if it was lying there in an extension of the line which connected us, or if the line struck her squarely at either a sharp or a flat angle.

The slot-machines were already crackling. Sharp bangs reverberated in a corner, followed by heavy explosions. A boy was bent over a dark screen already destroying cities with atom bombs in the early morning. He had carefully tended a small wound on his knee with a band-aid.

Suddenly I had tears in my eyes because I didn't have Sylvia with me to point that out to her. Some boy who throws real bombs on cities, I would have said, feels no different than this boy does now. She would have nodded, but only have half-understood what I meant and in any case she would not have been interested. But I was indifferent to that. It was not her intelligence and the depth of her interest in things that I loved, but that quality which did not have those characteristics but easily could have had them — that which remained when everything else had been taken away, that which I had already seen at first sight looking at her back.

In May we took the plane to Nice. The fight started while we were still in the air.

'Listen carefully Sylvia. Tonight it is too late, but tomorrow morning I'm going to see my mother. That's when she sits in the park by the sea. I'd rather you didn't go along.'

'Why not?'

'She wouldn't understand it any more than yours.'

'You don't have to tell her! We'll dig up some kind of story. I'm your assistant in the museum.'

'No Sylvia, we won't concoct any stories. Your stories bother me, we're not going to do that again.'

'You're ashamed of me.'

'I'm not at all ashamed of you, you know that very well. But for some reason or other you want to get my mother's attention.'

'Why should I?'

'Who knows. Because your own mother is not allowed to know that we live together even though your mother isn't at all old or sick.'

'No, but stupid, and that's worse.'

'In my opinion your mother isn't at all stupid. She loves you, and she would be quite capable of understanding this. She's a modern woman, but mine isn't; she got stuck somewhere thirty years ago.'

'Why do you suppose I don't want my mother to know?'

'You don't ever tell me anything about yourself, so how should I know? Perhaps because you can't admit to her that you are attracted to someone like her.'

'Oh, so you are my mother.'

'Except that I don't bother your father. In any case, I'm a woman too, and you're a pain in the neck. I never ask you anything, you force me to participate in a scandalous comedy for your mother, and now all I ask you is NOT to do something, and right away you refuse to go along with that. I was mad to take you with me.'

'You only took me with you so that you could forbid me to get to know your mother. That is your chief pleasure.'

I looked at her.

'When I listen to you.' I said, 'I feel as if I'm looking under a boulder in a damp garden and I see all those little beetles crawling around.'

Immediately I regretted that I had said that. Her soul was not as soft as her flesh and the stroking of her boyish hands; I don't know what kind of substance the soul is supposed to have, but hers reminded me of an egg: a hard white shell that didn't yield, but which could suddenly break, freeing a mass of amorphous slime.

'Why do you say such things?'

She broke. Her face dissolved into a bottomless anguish.

'You finally got me this far?' she sobbed.

Yes I finally had her that far, wanted to hold her in my arms as in the roadside restaurant the Swedish mothers held their infants. Suddenly she was part of me.

'What is it that bothers you? Tell me. Why are you so sad? It can't be because I said something nasty, because then you can hit me, or shrug your shoulders, or look out of the window. If you do, by the way, you'll see Paris down there. There's more, there's something else, tell me, what is it?'

She couldn't tell me, maybe she didn't know it herself. Crying she sat behind the plastic remains of her dinner, her face and neck covered with red spots.

'I'm taking the next plane back, I don't ever want to see you again.' Of course, I was afraid of that, but I didn't believe it would happen. Where would she go? Back to Petten? Besides I believed that somehow it unburdened her

whenever she was torn open like that. When we landed everything was okay again. It looked as if we were going to end up
in the sea, but at the last moment the tarmac was there. In
our hotel we took a bath, changed, and went on the
Promenade des Anglais to look at the sea and the stars and
the people. But the people looked at us too. Unceasingly we
were followed by all kinds of men under the palms, and
When we sat down on a terrace two immediately joined us at
our table. After their third word of French I said:

'It's alright if you speak Dutch.'

Their age was somewhere between Sylvia's and mine, and
it was clear that they had divided us beforehand, because one
started an exclusive conversation with me and the other with
Sylvia, in a first attempt to separate us. After some small
talk my partner said in a low voice:

'Maybe it sounds crazy, but as soon as I saw you I felt
that we had made this date a long time ago.'

'Are you serious?'

'If ever I were serious about anything it is this. I don't
know what it is, but it seems like I've know you for years. Do
you feel that way too?'

'A little perhaps.'

'You see, those things are never one-sided. When a hand
fits into a glove, then the glove fits the hand.'

He had his story well prepared, with comparisons and all,
and through frequent use he had it down pat. However, apart
from his story I did not dislike him, and I would have
preferred to tell him that he didn't need his story at all. But I
wasn't sure of that, after all he had more experience with
women than I. His friend meanwhile was whispering in
Sylvia's ear, and I would have enjoyed exchanging looks with
her, but she did not look at me.

'Maybe you think that I say this to any woman,' he said,
'but that's not true. I can't prove that, but you have to
believe me. You have to trust me a little.'

'Trust.' I said bitterly.

'Yes, I know what you mean. But you are not really talking to me but to someone else you know. You have to put that aside. Look where we are: that sea, that sky. A little trust, that's all I ask. When you cross the street then you trust that you're not going to get run over by some drunken idiot, right?'

'Right.'

'Well then.' Upon which he addressed himself to the group and said, 'I know of a good discotheque, let's go there.' His friend looked up annoyed; obviously he had not yet completed the first part of his repertoire. They got up to pay for the campari; just then I met Sylvia's eyes; she raised her eyebrows slightly — a sign which I didn't understand. We strolled into the busy lanes behind the boulevard in two groups. When I looked back I saw that Sylvia and her beau were lagging behind: that was also part of the strategy of course. I stopped but mine took my arm and said, 'Don't worry, they'll catch up.'

Even though we'd had a terrible quarrel a few hours ago, it didn't occur to me for a moment that she might want to take off with him; but I didn't feel like staying alone with my young man and I got tired of listening to his stories. When we were at the entrance of the discotheque the others arrived with their arms around each other, skipping.

Inside it was dark and filled with people and music. Old, tarred lifeboats hung from the ceiling above us. We sat on chairs with armrests made of thick, greasy rope. Sylvia drank too much and started to dance — in far too daring a fashion for my liking. It could only lead her partner to conclude that everything was going fine. I too drank a lot. Sometimes I thought of my mother who was asleep in her white bed, not far from here. When I didn't want to dance my escort started to work on me again.

'Let's get out of here. All those people. I want to be somewhere alone with you where we can talk in peace. Let's go to my hotel room. Don't worry, I won't rape you. After all, we don't have to go to bed right away? We're not in a hurry are we? We'll get to bed eventually. Shall I promise you that I won't go to bed with you tonight? Scout's honour.'

Suddenly I didn't see Sylvia any more. I got up to look for her, followed by my partner who thought I was preceding him to his hotel.

'Just a minute,' he called, while he frantically tried to get the attention of the waiter in his striped blue and white T-shirt.

I found her between the rope ladders and fishnets which separated the bar.

'Let's go,' I said.

'Yes,' she answered and waved goodbye to her friend like a child, 'bye bye.'

'What?' he called, his eyes suddenly bulging.

But that was the end of his script and instead he flung his glass of whisky into her face. At the same time mine gave me a hard slap. Right away others became involved, and while we quickly got out of there I heard my one calling:

'Bitches! dirty bitches! Ce sont lesbiennes!'

In the earsplitting silence of the street we ran hand in hand to our hotel, choking with laughter.

'There she is.'

I pointed to my mother — in the distance with her back to us under trees, in a reclining chair. Last year it had still been a straightback canvas chair. The chair stood on the grass behind a bench where a nurse was reading a book.

'Is she that rich?'

'She has my father's pension. He was a professor. He also wrote several books and they're still being sold.'

'Does she get money for that?'

'From each book she gets a few guilders. So, Sylvia, be nice and wait near the fountain while I go and talk with her for a while. Or walk to the sea, then I'll see you later at the hotel but be careful that you don't run into those men.'

'Which fountain? It's loaded with fountains here.'

'That big one over there, with the three Graces.'

Slowly I walked down the path towards my mother. Not a leaf stirred and under the trees it was so comforting that I felt as if I were walking inside my own body. Near the bench I stopped and looked at the back of her head, — that was the last time I would see her. The nurse looked at me, her eyes still reflecting the images from the book. If I now close my eyes and concentrate on that look it seems I should be able to figure out what she was reading. It had something to do with CRINOLINE something swishing, somewhere around 1840: LA CHARTREUSE DE PARME perhaps. I nodded at her, walked around the bench and stood in front of my mother. She was looking up into the leaves, her hands folded in her lap in a way that I had never seen her do before. It was as if she had put them away, the way one puts away a book.

Very slowly her eyes turned down and looked at me. The expression did not change, that is to say, they did not express anything. I smiled at her — only then did she see it was me.

'Hello mama. It's really me.'

'I was dreaming,' she said, 'but I didn't believe it was true.' She smiled and raised herself slightly. 'When did you come? Give me a kiss.' I pressed my lips on the cool, thin skin of her cheeks. The nurse had turned around and I told her who I was. She whispered that I should not make it very long because the patient was very weak. I sat down in the grass and put my arms around my knees. Beside the chair lay a cane. I smiled at her again because I didn't know what to say really.

'You look better than the last time,' she said. 'Are you happy?'

'Yes,' I smiled, 'Very.'

'You have a friend?'

I nodded. I remember even now that I not only nodded with my head but with my entire upper body.

'I'm so happy for you. What's his name?'

'Thomas,' I said, 'Thomas Nithart.'

'How old is he?'

'Let's not talk about me, mama, but about you. If he were sixty, or twenty, I would still love him.'

She was silent and for a while looked past me.

Then she asked, 'What does he do for a living?'

'Oh, don't always fuss about such things. Even if he were, I don't know. . . some superintendent somewhere. I am thirty five, I know very well what I'm doing. I'm very happy, much happier than with Alfred. By the way, he asked me to say hello to you.'

'Why didn't he come with you?'

'Alfred?'

'No, Thomas, your Thomas. What does his family do?'

'Dear mama, please.'

'As you like.'

She didn't say anything further, but I knew she already
had her doubts. Perhaps the umbilical cord between a mother
and a child is never really broken. When I went to bed with a
boy for the first time I was seventeen, and the next morning
at the breakfast table my father took off his glasses, inclined
his head slightly and said,

'Good morning.'

He put his glasses on again and went on reading the paper.
But my mother kept looking at me and said nothing. I fled
past her:

'Why are you looking at me like that?'

The morning sun shone on the rose breakfast dishes — and
then she broke a cup. My father took his glasses off again and
looked with amazement at the pieces on her plate. Perhaps
her understanding consisted merely of breaking the cup,
perhaps it was not the result of something, of a thought or a
suspicion, but her understanding lay simply in her body, in
the hand which let go of the cup.

For half an hour or so we spoke about other things. But
just as the nurse turned around to warn me with her index
finger on her wristwatch, my mother asked:

'Do you know that boy?'

'Which boy?'

She looked past me and I turned around. On the lawn
stood Sylvia in her white trousers, basketball shoes and an
old shirt of Alfred's. When she saw us looking at her she
walked over to us. I paled with annoyance and I saw that my
mother noticed.

'Hey!' she called out, 'that's a coincidence, how did you
happen to be in Nice?'

'Hello,' said I, 'how did you get here?' and then made my
second blunder: 'This is Sylvia, mama. Sylvia Nit. . . no, sorry
Potmans.' How horrifying. Freud would have been in stitches
had he been there.

'Your daughter has told me so much about you,' Sylvia
said to my mother. 'I'm her neighbour. I heard that your

husband was a professor and that he wrote books which are still being sold. I'd like to read them sometimes. Do you know that I. . .'

But while she was still talking something ghastly happened. My mother took her cane and raised herself, shaking, and with the cane began to beat Sylvia in the way one strikes a mad dog. With one jump Sylvia was out of reach of the cane. My mother swung once more in my direction, dropped the cane in the grass and stood there shaking with her hands in the air, like a blind person who has been the victim of a cruel game. I had jumped up, not believing what was happening, utterly devastated. The nurse, who had no idea what was going on, had run up and put her arm around my mother's shoulders. I yelled:

'Goddammit, goddammit, mama! Isn't she a human being? Didn't I tell you that I am happy, goddammit?'

I felt my face contort, I cried, but I also realized that everywhere around us old faces had turned our way; it became even quieter in the park. The nurse had grabbed the cane and led mother away up the path. I stared at her back.

'Go talk to her,' said Sylvia. 'You must go and talk to her.'

'No, I won't, to hell with it, I won't. Come along.' I put my arm around her.

'But perhaps it was only because I said something about your father.'

'No, for god's sake, come.'

We walked in the direction of the sea. I had noticed that the nurse had forgotten her book on the bench, but it was upside down.

My father said:

'You watch. When you are writing something and you put down your pen briefly, observe how it lies. If you've put it down with the point away from you that's a sign you're involved in a good way. If it points at you then something isn't right. Then it's better to stop.'

Now and then I put my pen down and carefully walk to the window. When I lean out over the windowsill I look into a ravine. I don't think I have ever seen such a big hole. It lies still in the heat of the afternoon. Pneumatic drills, deserted trucks everywhere. The bulldozers immobile against the mass of stone as if overcome by a natural disaster, their necks broken, their chins against the ground.

On the other side of the hole there stands, lies, exists, the Palais des Papes as a giant, deserted cocoon, from which a fearful insect has emerged and now somewhere in the world lies dying with its feet in the air. Apparently the building has been sandblasted not long ago because it looks like new. The stones have the same yellowish colour as the rock. Someone might think that the castle had emerged from that hole. There, on the other side, is my car too.

In a year a large, sundrenched square, will once again be under this window, but under it will be a parking place for the haute volé who attend the performances in the courtyard of the palace in evening dress.

My room is furnished in the neo-gothic style of about 1890 with furniture which so far I've only seen at French fleamarkets. The bed, the chairs, the spooky buffet, everything is black, high, pointed, turned wood; on the wall is a framed reproduction of the Fragonard's reading girl, the only colour in the room. All the hotels were full and I was glad to get this room. Besides the old lady is very kind. She got the writing paper for me, and every time when she brings me food or makes the bed, she asks if I feel alright or if she shouldn't call a doctor. But after I had slept twelve hours I felt much better and when I sit still I don't notice anything. Only when I go to the bathroom, or walk to the window, then it starts again.

Occasionally at night in bed I hear an owl in the distance, near the Rhone.

'Why did you separate from Alfred?'

It was Sunday morning and we were still in bed. In the daylight her eyes were green, by artificial light they became blue. Outside the city remained quiet.

'Because we weren't able to have children.'

'Whose fault was it?'

'Mine, because he has two children now.'

'Didn't you want kids?'

'There's nothing I wanted more. I tried everything but the whole thing was hopelessly plugged. It was depressing as hell, having my period show up every month and being with a man who like me definitely wanted children.

She sat up.

'Is motherhood for you the highest calling for a woman?'

'Sylvia, you know me better than that? Of course not. But it is for a daughter. If you always think of yourself as a daughter then there is only one way to get rid of your mother, and that is by becoming a mother yourself.'

She lay down again.

'It seems to me you don't love children at all. For you children are only a way to get rid of your mother.'

I didn't say anything.

'And if you had had a child,' said she, 'would you have loved it then?'

'Yes,' I said, 'Because the moment it was born I would have had nothing to do with my mother. You are right, I don't love children, but I would have loved that special child, not as a daughter but as a mother.'

'And if it had been switched after it was born?'

'Then I would have loved that child. Naturally! If that wasn't the case a man would never be able to love his child.'

'Why not?'

'Because he is never as sure that the child is really his as his wife who knows that the child is really hers. A woman can always make a small slip, and then she might not know which man's child this is, but she does know it is hers.'

'Men always have to go on faith,' she laughed. 'They're helplessly delivered into our hands.'

I laughed too.

'Precisely, helpless, that is what they are. Look at their nipples for example. We don't have anything quite as ridiculous on our bodies.' I was getting carried away and enjoying it: 'Do you know what it is about us women? We are much more open to the world. Men have only nine openings in their body, we have twelve.'

'Twelve?' She started to count: her eyes, her ears, one two, three, four, her nostrils, her mouth, five, six, seven, her nipples, eight, nine, she turned the sheet down, her vagina, her anus, ten, eleven. 'I don't get further than eleven.'

'Yes,' I said, then you have that in common with very young boys who also think that pee and babies come out of the same hole.'

'Oh, that's right too.'

I pressed my index finger into her navel.

'Our thirteenth opening, for the man the tenth, is permanently closed.'

I had said it very solemnly, and by the tone of my own voice I was overcome by a strange emotion — I suddenly saw an amazing image: all the women, connected by an ancient, uninterrupted, ongoing, multi-branched umbilical cord. Whereas men were attached like loose ends, fringes.

Sylvia pulled the sheets up again.

'Did Alfred love children?'

I shrugged.

'I don't know if that was it. I think he really wanted to

verify that it wasn't his fault. In the end it just didn't work any more. A marriage without children becomes a risky affair in the long run. A child binds two people, but at the same time is an isolator. Arguments are less likely to flare up because you must take the child into account, if only not waken it. Without a child everything becomes much more vehement. If you want to, you can separate any moment.

'Like in our case, you mean.'

I glanced at her.

'Like with us,' said I. 'But there's the other aspect which is that without a child you give the relationship your undivided attention.'

She turned on her side, her back to me. The turn of the conversation bothered me, but I didn't know what to say.

After a while she said:

'So you really never got rid of your mother.'

Right away I saw my mother's back again, on the path in the Jardin du Roi Albert I, the nurse's arm around her shoulders. I did not follow her. I had spent the rest of the morning lying on the beach, exhausted. Sylvia had done it. It should have never been allowed to happen like that, but it did happen. I had not visited her again; the same afternoon we had rented a car and driven into France, using secondary roads, eating where it seemed best and sleeping wherever we happened to end up. Until Paris. Beautiful days – always with the image of this old woman suddenly flailing around her with a cane, at the end of her life. But even since we got back I had not written her. I had the barbaric feeling that I had to offer her on the altar of Sylvia.

She was still lying with her back to me. When I did not answer she asked:

'Would you like me to have a child by you?'

With my arms under my head I looked at the Japanese drawing of a woman who washes herself in the stream, under a branch of blossoms. I realized immediately that our relationship had reached a critical stage. A child. Sooner or later it had to get to that point; I had known her for four months, I had really expected it much sooner. Each of us were only lesbian in that we slept together, but neither of us were women who got sick at the idea of having to sleep with a man. We never went to cafés or clubs for homosexuals, or to one of those women ghettos which could be found in the city, and as far as I was concerned, I knew for certain that there would never be another woman in my life except her. What could I say? I could no more give her a child than have one myself.

'We could adopt a child, if you like.'

'That's not what I asked,' she said. 'I asked if you would like to have a child by me.'

'Yes,' I said. 'Of course. But that's not possible.'

She was quiet after that. When I thought she had gone back to sleep, she said:

'When I was about fourteen I once walked into the sea. At our place on the beach in Petten. I don't remember it myself, but my father told me. I went up the dyke, then down the dyke, I walked straight ahead, over the beach and then into the sea, between the breakwaters. I was fully dressed, I think I had just come out of the house, and I walked until the water was over my head. I know how to swim, but I didn't then. Beachcombers hauled me out of the water. They applied artificial respiration, I was half frozen, because it was November.'

The story scared me.

'Why did you do that?'

'I don't know.'

'Why are you telling it to me now?'

'I don't know.'

I took her in my arms, I was worried, I felt disaster and suddenly tears came into my eyes.

'Are you crying?' she asked.

I pressed her against me. Never had I been so close to something which I did not understand, that thing in her which attracted me. But I also had the feeling that it would be finished between us the moment it really became visible. There was something which she knew herself and which she kept from me, it was what she was, something that could not be put into words but which only could be shown. I wished that I was less close to it, but knew that in any case I would never get closer to it than now.

She fell asleep in my arms.

After Compiègne the same car stayed in my rearview mirror. What a nuisance to have someone continually breathing down your neck. It was a white Citroen with a man behind the wheel. Whenever I accelerated, he did too. When I reduced speed, so did he. I don't think that he had any designs on me because he could only see the back of my head. I think he was simply absent minded and stayed in my wake; I had become his leader. Near Paris where the highway continually splits off towards assorted medieval gates, I finally lost him, thank goodness!

Because I always forget how to drive around the city I suddenly found myself in narrow streets, between vegetable stalls and an overpass where a train thundered across. After much asking, I finally drove across the Pont des Arts and from there I once more knew the way. I parked the car and ate lunch on a terrace overlooking the Seine and the Louvre.

With Sylvia I had repeated the visit which I had once made with my father. I was still a child and it was my first visit to Paris with my parents. My father said that all things contained in the museum could be lined up between two points. The first was the Nike of Samothrace at the entrance, its marble blowing in the wind, a white ecstatic apparition from another world, and at the same time the victory of the hand over the stone, inaudibly jubilant because of the shuffling in the stairwell. The other point lay deep in the museum, in the Assyrian collection, hundreds of meters further on. My mother had stopped at the renaissance.

The obelisk of Hammurabi. A black, slender, gleaming stone, higher than a man.

'Do you see that it is an index finger?'

In the nearly four thousand years that this stone had existed, my father was perhaps the first to notice that: it has the form of a raised index finger, the warning finger of the law. I knew that finger – ever since Miss Borst. In place of the nail is the image of the king. Standing, he receives the law from the sun god who sits on a throne. Underneath, on the flesh, are hundreds of articles carved in glistening cuneiform characters.

I remember one which my father had told me about, and I recalled it for Sylvia:

'Should the builder build a house which falls down and kills the occupant then the builder shall be killed; should the son of the occupant be killed, then the son of the builder will be killed.'

'Hammurabi was crazy,' said Sylvia. 'The son can't help it that his father is a bungler?'

'But the son of the occupant died too without being guilty?'

'Well? Isn't one enough?'

She didn't come back to the subject of a child, which we had discussed that Sunday morning, and I didn't either, although I sometimes had an urge to. I had the feeling that something was smouldering there that should definitely be smothered before it set everything on fire; but on the other hand I was afraid that by bringing it up again I would rekindle it and then perhaps could not control it any more.

Shortly after that I read an interview in the paper with a writer whose play was to have its première at the beginning of the Holland Festival. That was in June. He said that the Greeks always had women's roles played by men disguised as women. It was an established social convention. Of course Queens like Clytaemnestra or Jocasta were always intended as women, but as long as this custom existed, right up to the renaissance, the authors had, according to him, also deliberately used it to enable a double meaning and had intended it as it was actually done: the 'women' then were not women, but men, transvestites. As far as the Greeks were concerned, there really were no regular women: they were something like today's electronic kitchen apparatus cum incubator. Love between people existed exclusively between men: when Plato in his Symposium speaks about love he refers to homosexual love. That's why he, this author, had decided to portray the myth of Orpheus and Eurydice as the story of two men. In this he felt a sense of support from most ancient story of man, the Epic of Gilgamesch, in which a man goes to seek his friend in the underworld.

'Do you feel like going there?' I asked Sylvia.

I thought perhaps the play could provide some kind of

perspective to the situation that we ourselves were in; perhaps we could talk about the play afterwards, while in reality it would be about us. In that way it could be kept under control.

It was her first première and she made a dress of black silky linen. But in the lobby of the theatre it was evident that we were   not the only ones who had received the message. The most elegant homos of the city were there, – the elder ones carefully coiffed above their seamed faces with ocasionally a red-lined cape over their shoulders, the younger ones with long blonde tresses, and see-through lace shirts open down to their navels, jewelry dangling in their breast hair and their eyes everywhere except on the person they were with. Several were in the company of conspicuous, fat old ladies who walked with difficulty; some alone: dapper with a shoulder bag and a billiard cue in their back so that it seemed they did not walk but moved into the theatre on a conveyor belt, and then of course others who were not obvious. There were few lesbians as far as I could tell.

I felt there was some tension in the house. I pointed out to Sylvia the artistically well-known who usually sat in clusters, and the industrial moguls with their entourage of choreographers, interior designers, fashion designers, surrounded by mannequins who looked as if they were blind. Sylvia merely nodded, but I could see she was impressed. In a dark side-box sat the playright; I remembered him from when I was still married.

'Watch,' I said, when the first bell rang, 'here comes Alfred.' At that moment he entered with his wife. I suddenly felt a strange kind of emotion which surprised me. She preceded him to the second seat of the third row: where I had sat for seven years during every première. Alfred himself sat on the aisle, near the door, so he could easily get away.

'Is that him? That tall one?'

Sylvia craned her neck, but the light had already started to fade.

Right away the first scene received a spontaneous applause: a stylized whitish forest against a dark background; in one tree hung the gold coloured hide of a ram. Music sounded and the Argonauts came on fighting, their swords dripping blood. The dragon was slain and they looked up to the Golden Fleece. The entire performance was very stylized; the director had, wisely, been less inspired by the Greeks than by the neo-classicists. Under this tree Orpheus then tells about Eurydice who is waiting for him and has been promised to him if he brings home the Golden Fleece. With all those men there you really got the idea that there were no women in the world.

The second scene was applauded too: a highly romantic, arched little bridge, backlighted in flat white, overgrown by ivy and flanked by two weathered, mossgrown garden vases which held a profusion of hanging flowers and fruit. The homecoming of Orpheus, the Golden Fleece over his shoulder. I loved every part of it but of course I'm a sucker for almost anything that happens on stage. Eurydice was more devastatingly beautiful than any woman ever could have been, just as a boy soprano or a counter tenor is always more affecting than a soprano. The death scene caused by a snake-bite was followed by their mating, after which Eurydice fell onto Orpheus' sword, and the silence was notable when, for the first time in the Stadsschouwburg Theatre, you could see a spectacle which until then could only have been found in the sex theatres. The festival audience could see the prodigious fluid flying through the air in flashing arches. For a moment it troubled me to see shed on the stage, for artistic reasons, that fluid which by its absence was threatening to become a problem for Sylvia and myself. I suddenly also realized that all the whitish costumes and sets were the colour of sperm.

Intermission.

'Hello,' said Alfred in the crowd near the buffet. He had a cup of coffee in each hand.

'This is Alfred,' I said. 'This is Sylvia.'

He reached out his little finger to her.

'Hello Sylvia,' he said kindly, and to me: 'There's going to be a small party afterwards. If you feel like it, come. It's upstairs.'

Beside me a young man with a belligerent angelface had overheard the invitation. 'Does the great criticus favour a celebration — or perhaps a crucifixion?' Alfred smirked and said: 'Bye.'

'Bye,' said I.

I had to laugh. Since my divorce I was no longer accustomed to this kind of atmosphere. Everything was still the same as always: only young and old people talked about the play, the rest watched each other or talked about very different things. A lady said:

'I hope for the sake of those two poor boys that the play won't have a long run.'

'Yes, and with a Sunday matinee,' laughed her husband. 'But perhaps they learn that at drama school.'

'Would you be interested in taking one of those courses, Jan-Willem?'

When we walked near the author's colleagues, we only heard comments like 'Bunch of garbage,' 'Sensationalism,' or 'Disaster,' or 'A waste of time.' Nothing had changed. I didn't get a chance to talk with Sylvia about the play because I constantly ran into people I had not seen for years. Sylvia was eyed with interest, but that bothered me less than when someone didn't remember me or pretended not to. In any case, now the whole city knew it, and it gave me a sense of relief.

Finally the bell rang and we were alone again.

'Do you want to go to that party afterwards?' I asked as we walked back to our seats.

'It's up to you.'

After my last telephone conversation with Alfred I really didn't feel like it, but that didn't affect Sylvia. Besides he had been very nice and perhaps it was good for her to meet some people. After half a year she really knew no one but me.

The Hades. All black against a white background, — the negative of the spermatic world of the living. Pluto was not mollified by song but by a rhyming poem in which Orpheus describes his sadness. The dead Eurydice appeared without wig and glued-on eyelashes and looked what he really was: a boy. Orpheus looks back, his friend disappears. Thereupon his destruction by the Bacchantes, played by his friends from the first act, now as transvestites.

There were few shouts of approval, but the playwright could not complain about the applause. Awkward and shy he appeared from between the wings. The two leading characters took him by the hand and led him beaming and with expansive motions to the footlights, like their retarded little boy.

'How did you like it?'

Between the portraits of actors — still radiating their fantastic, hollow power even when long dead — Sylvia and I slowly walked to the upstairs foyer.

'I don't know. Quite nice, and you?'

From anyone else a vague answer like that would have annoyed me, but not from her.

'Did you recognize anything of our situation in it?'

'Of us?' She looked at me astonished. 'But which of us is in the underworld?'

I smiled and silently took her hand.

You, I thought. You are in the underworld, because you are a ghost — not of someone dead, but of an unborn.

In the foyer a band played nostalgic melodies from around the turn of the century, which must have resounded at the cradle of my parents. The large doors to the balcony were open. In the centre stood the mayor with the director of the theatre, and from a corner Alfred motioned. He introduced Sylvia to Karin, his wife, bad tempered as usual. I had to sit on the sofa beside her.

'Don't forget about the babysitter,' she said to Alfred.

'I'll phone in a minute.'

'That won't help, he has to leave before twelve.'

'When it's time you had better go ahead.'

'Yes, that's the usual procedure.' And to me: 'It's a

student — he has an exam tomorrow.'

I nodded.

'Shall I get something to drink?' asked Alfred. He took our
orders and went to the long table which was loaded with
filled glasses.

He won't be back, I thought.

'He won't be back,' said Karin. 'How are you these days?'

'Excellent,' I said and smiled in Sylvia's direction but she
was rolling a cigarette, facing the hall.

'You're looking very well. Have you changed your hair?'

'I don't think so. But it gets more regular care these days.'

Alfred was already back with the drinks, even shaking off
someone who excitedly had tried to tell him something.

'That guy wanted to tell me what to put in my piece,' he
said.

'What did you think of it?'

'Now you want ME to tell you?'

'A woman's judgement is invaluable for a piece such as
this.'

And to Sylvia: 'How did you feel about it?'

Sylvia nodded. I didn't like the innuendo very much, but I
decided to keep it light. Beside it may not have been an
innuendo at all.

'But you never ask me,' said Karin.

'We have a different kind of contact, love.'

'Indeed.'

'According to me,' I said, 'he could just as easily have
made Orpheus a woman as Eurydice a man.'

That comment was of course more for Sylvia's benefit
than Alfred's, — moreover I really wondered if that was true.
Alfred had his glass at his mouth, but then put it down without taking a sip.

'Precisely,' he said. 'That would have been easy. Except
that it would not have fitted with his point of departure: it
lies in the history of the theatre, and not in the theatre itself.
He should have written an essay about it, he should have shown

for example that Shakespeare used transvestites to deal with certain taboos. The whole question of double impersonation, — women dressed as men: originally they would have been male actors, playing the role of a woman pretending to be a man, so that you had a kind of man with a double bottom. Some day I'll write a book about the influence of the theatre. Conventions on the theatre. Your own father had a better understanding how to approach this kind of thing.'

'Thank you,' I said, as if I were my father. 'But I don't agree with you. I thought it was a beautiful performance.'

'You know,' he said addressing himself to Sylvia, 'the tragedy must be seen as a paradox. A tragedy consists of two truths which contradict each other. In ordinary life the truth is opposite the lie. All truths cover each other or are continuations of each other; they can never contradict each other. The fact that right now it is not raining outside does not contradict the fact that we are having a very pleasant little chat here.'

'A pleasant little chat he calls that,' said Karin.

'No,' said Sylvia.

'But in the tragedy human truth is opposed to divine truth, and it's this contradiction that kills the hero, pulls him apart. Orpheus is pulled apart, Oedipus pokes his eyes out.'

'His eyes?'

At the door there was a small burst of applause. The author entered, now suddenly with excited dance steps, followed by the actors, their hair still wet from the shower. A little self-consciously the mayor looked at the two boys who before the intermission had jacked each other off; but also appeared a little proud because he had not banned the performance. The author walked over to his friends who stood up and embraced him.

'Is that his girlfriend?' asked Sylvia, when she saw that he went to sit down on the sofa with his arm around a young woman. 'But isn't that guy a homo?'

Alfred laughed.

'Obviously you're the only one who hasn't been to bed

with him.'

'Then why does he write such a crazy play?'

'I suspect there are many people who at this point are wondering about that,' said Alfred, while he looked at me.

'What were you trying to say with your story about the tragedy?' I asked.

'Story about the tragedy? Yes, I was trying to make the point that in the human world a reflection of these two truths can only be found in the fact that there are men and women. Historically of course it's the other way, but if you put together a play with only men or only women, then you can never have a real tragedy, only at best various melodramatic situations to which you can give an attractive wrapping. That's what we saw tonight. The dragon behind the stage was the leading person.'

Was he still speaking about the theatre? Was I the princess on the lesbian pea, or was he saying in a round-about way that a woman with a woman and a man with a man could not signify anything, not outside the theatre either? As if the greatest experience in life was the whole business of being-pulled-apart, the great tragedy, which presumably then would have to be hailed in his marriage with Karin. I decided to let the matter rest and not try for further clarification, because before I knew it I would be making the kind of statements that would ruin Sylvia's evening.

It had become crowded and hot. The dressers and stage-hands had arrived, the mayor had left and some young actors of the company started to dance in the style of their grand-parents. The author spotted me from far away and waved. I put my hands together and shook them above my head. He saluted, and when he stood up to come over and see me, I stood up too and walked toward him. I knew what he wanted — everything just like before.

I got a kiss on my cheek.

'What a long time! You and Alfred back together?'

'Please.'

'What did he think of it?'

When I made a face, he said:

'I guess so. Give me a piece of paper and I'll write down exactly what he's going to write, and you? Remember, tonight only compliments.'

'I thought it was an immortal masterpiece.'

'Finally a woman with the ability to understand.'

Curious he looked past me. 'Who's that girl?'

'A friend of mine,' I said without looking back.

'You don't suppose you could introduce me?'

'I wouldn't dream of it.'

Sylvia put her hand on my shoulder.

'I'm hot, I'm going out on the balcony for a minute.'

'If it's permitted I'm going too,' said Alfred, and coolly to the author: 'Hello.'

'You go ahead,' I said, 'I'll be there in a minute.'

'That's how it goes,' said the author. Functionaries are allowed, but artists aren't. Artists have to eat in the kitchen, with the hired help.' He laughed and shook my hand. 'See you again in another ten years.'

'Good luck!'

When I saw Karin sitting alone on the sofa something prompted me to sit beside her for a moment.

'They're on the balcony,' she said.

It was crowded on the balcony. I saw then standing together, leaning against the railing and it pleased me to see them talking together. It seemed that the breach in my life was built over and it had regained some kind of unity. Karin started to complain again, about the babysitter, about theatre life, and about the inadequacy of everything in general. She was able to have children, yes, but that seemed to be the extent of it. I limited myself to nodding and saying yes.

'I must go,' she said after five minutes or so and got up. 'Say hello to Alfred for me.'

'We'll be leaving soon too.'

I ambled over to the balcony. Down below was the busy square in the summer evening.

'Karin said to say hello for her, Alfred. She went home.'

'Yes,' he said, 'the babysitter.'

'Do you want to stay longer?' I asked Sylvia.

'I'm ready to go home.'

'You wouldn't bother dancing as in Nice?'

'You were in Nice?' asked Alfred. 'How is your mother?'

For a moment I didn't know what to say. Sylvia turned with a quick movement and leaned over the railing.

'I told her you said hello.'

'Is there something wrong with her?'

'Goodbye,' said Sylvia suddenly and held out her hand. 'See you.'

'See you, Sylvia,' said Alfred.

When I let her go out ahead of me and looked back at Alfred, he put up his thumb and pulled a face which expressed admiring congratulations.

I smiled, flattered.

A few days later in the museum I showed Sylvia the icons. The museum was located in a patrician home on the Keizersgracht, where the Zinnicq-Bergmann collection took up two floors. He had been an older friend of my father's and he offered the job to me when I was still with Alfred; I accepted it because I didn't want to sit at home all day. The basement suite was used by Mr. and Mrs. Roebljov. Mr. Roebljov, now in his eighties, had also been brought from St. Petersburg by Zinnicq Bergmann after his pre-revolution position there as ambassador. There were all kinds of juicy stories about the diplomat and his young Russian; but after the death of his master the servant had married a Dutch woman who looked much more Russian than he. Upstairs at the front was the room of the administrator who came in once a week; my room looked out on the garden.

'Mrs. Roebljov — Miss Nithart.'

Mrs. Roebljov, or Roebljova, whom we met in the basement, did something very strange when she shook hands with Sylvia: she made a small curtsy and then right away went on with her sweeping. I could only explain it by assuming that she disapproved of our relationship and that she tried to hide this through a curtsy. People always betray themselves most obviously in the way they don't want to betray themselves.

Upstairs, under the baroque stucco of the high hall we found Mr. Roebljov at his little table reading the paper.

'This is Miss Nithart, Mr. Roebljov, my friend.'

He quickly took off his glasses, put the paper down, stood up and greeted her courteously. That evening, during supper, he would almost certainly tell his wife that he thought she was a very nice girl and that everybody should lead his own life; upon which she would possibly say: — Better be silent, Andrej. Better be silent.

'Has anybody been in today?'

'Not yet, madam,' It still sounded like njet after all those years. Gallantly he handed the pen to Sylvia and let her sign the opened guestbook.

With Sylvia it seemed to me that the silence of the museum was even deeper than normal. Our heels clicked on the marble, but when we went inside the rooms even that noise disappeared. We stopped. On the red-silken wallpaper the icons glowed as windows to a motionless, golden world.

Once I had been here as a child. Everywhere there were large easy chairs and tables; the icons I can't remember very well, but I can still see the cheerful little gods and the vines of the grape on the soft green ceiling. In one corner of the room with his back to the window sat the ancient Zinnicq-Bergmann, a rug over his knees and a wine red skullcap on head; his face with the large moustache in the shadow. Tea was brought on a silver tray by the same Roebljov, then a man in the prime of his life, dressed in a loose Russian shirt with a belt around it. I was about five and in my memory my father makes a little dance for a somber-looking Zinnicq-Bergmann, on tiptoes, his hands high above his head in the form of a bird, while my mother leans against the sofa her arms spread over the back, crooning, her head relaxed. But it probably wasn't that way at all.

Where once there was a long table with large sheets of paper, etchings perhaps, the Carceri of Piranesi I imagine, there are now display cases with equipment necessary for icon painting: brushes, paint, wood, chisels, blue, chalk, leafgold, pitch. Also photographs of monks painting on mount Athos, and of icons in places where they belonged, in churches, in the Soviet Union and the Balkan countries, taken by me.

'They could be dolls,' said Sylvia.

'You are standing among the saints. Don't compare icons with saintly pictures in catholic churches. They're not merely images of saints, they themselves are saints.'

'But how can that be; they're not alive?'

I looked at her.

'Do you still remember that once we gave a picture to your mother and you're on that picture with a certain boy in a reptile house? Then you gave that picture a kiss.'

She turned away.

'Thomas,' she said.

Slowly she started to walk along the icons. Near the master-piece of the collection, the Annunciation of Oestjoeg, from the Novgorod school, she stopped. A little later she sat down under it, on the floor. She stretched her legs, leaned with her head against the wall and closed her eyes.

'In Petten I lived right behind the dyke,' she said. 'That's where I was born. When I looked out of the window or when I came out of the house, I always saw that dyke. It is higher than our house and it was as if the horizon was twenty meters away. A dead straight horizon of stone. In the summer there were usually people on it, from the camp-ground close by, but the rest of the year it was empty. You can hardly hear the sea, but when you climb to the top of the dyke it suddenly roars like an animal with mean teeth, and the wind blasts in your face. Always wind, wind, and that damned dyke. Something like this,' she went on and opened her eyes, 'simply isn't there. In fact, there you can't even imagine that it exists. As a small girl I used to think: later I will live some place where it never blows, and where you never see such a long, straight line of stone. Just behind the village the dyke changes into dunes again, that was my favorite spot. You could really see how beautiful and old the dunes are. Maybe you think it's crazy if I say this, but when I saw your mother with that white nurse walking away from us I suddenly had to think of that spot. Do you think that's silly?'

'No,' I said. I was quite moved. She had never talked that long before.

'You got me out of that place. That's not why I love you, but without you I'd still be there. I love you, you know that? I've never said that to anyone before. I will always love you, you won't forget that? Even when we have a fight, and when you say terrible things to me, then that still has nothing to do with my loving you. That's much deeper. I can't say how deep.'

In the hall I heard Mr. Roebljov talking to someone.

'You're sweet,' I said. 'But now you have to get up, there is a visitor.'

The nameless landscapes. The slopes and valleys which will all have different names and a history; where the soil differs and has been explored by farmers and scientists and put on a map; where the grapes differ and the wines; country roads with names where for centuries one event has followed another; the plains where the battles were fought, people hit by arrows and cannon-balls; villages which became worlds: — everything slid past in a languid stream. One landscape replaced another, already forgotten, like faces on a busy street. It was still overcast, but much warmer, the insects which burst against my windshield increased in number and became gradually larger. Some were gruesome yellow splashes.

When in the afternoon near Avallon I filled up the petrol tank and had the slaughter on my window washed off I went into the roadside restaurant to have another cup of coffee. The first person I saw sitting at a table was the author of ORPHEUS' FRIEND. He was so tanned his blue eyes seemed bleached.

'Fancy seeing you here,' he said and stood up. 'On holiday?'

Because I didn't think it necessary to burden him with my deceased mother I nodded.

'Where?'

'In Nice.'

'In August in Nice? Don't you go crazy there?'

'It just so happened, and you?'

'I'm on my way home. I left the day after the première and I've been working for two months in a secret Italian mountain village. Half of it is ruins, and the other half old people. Great, no paper, no radio, no traffic, no nothing. Has anything happened in Amsterdam?'

Did anything happen in Amsterdam?

'You didn't miss a thing,' said I.

'Two months ago we saw each other last, but I have the feeling that it's more like ten years.'

'Yes,' I said, 'me too.'

'Your feared ex-husband wrote a rather unfavourable review which I read just before I left the next day. A dud, he called it.'

'Just forget it. I'm sure he would have rather written your play than his review.'

'According to him I had blocked myself from understanding the nature of tragedy. As if whatever the reviewers think of in an hour I haven't already thought of a hundred times, but had obvious reasons to reject. It would be better to guess those reasons. You wonder why they don't do it themselves if they know so much about it.'

'Seems like it really bothers you. Of course he wanted to be a writer himself.'

'Really?'

'What do you think? Don't be naive. Anyhow, that's why you're a writer I guess. He had criticized everything to pieces before he even started. Sometimes he would tell me about an idea, but the next day he had already decided it wouldn't work, or that someone else had done it before.'

'Which is possible. But you only know that after you've done it. You always have to do something first. Then leave it alone for the moment or else you can't transcend it.'

'Not what?'

'Transcend, transcend your own intentions. From the day comes the night, your own night, where no one else has been. I just finished writing a novel all at one go, but I have no idea what it portrays. At home I'll type it out, and then I'll start having a critical look at it. If you start with the criticism then you're like a man who eats a turd in the hope that he'll shit a loaf of bread.'

'Not bad.'

'Speaking about a turd, I remember making up a poem about him.'

'He seems to inspire you.'

'Resistance always inspires,' he said and leafed through a greasy blue notebook. 'But you have to be careful you don't end up writing for the evil minded. Here it is.

Reviewer: A.B. gobbles my cuisine
and next day produces
his reviewing turd:
'You should smell it,'
he pronounces blandly,
and he thinks he's a gourment cook.'

'Are you going to publish that?' I asked.

'Perhaps. In the corner of some magazine or other. Why?'

The waitress came and I ordered coffee.

'Do you know,' he said, 'that I often find myself thinking of that girl who was with you that time?'

I had to control myself a little when I looked at him.

'Why?'

'You know that feeling, when you look at someone, without at that moment paying much attention, but later the person keeps coming back to you. Just as if it was more than an ordinary face, more like a landscape.'

'What kind of landscape did you see in hers?' I suddenly didn't feel very well, I was a little scared of what he was going to say.

'I have to think about that,' he said and closed his eyes. His chin rested on his hands and his mouth was slightly open, as if he could think better when he didn't breathe through his nose. Slowly he said: 'I saw her sitting there, behind you. . . then she stood up and said something to you. . . then she went away. . .'

'To the balcony.'

'She looked at me for one moment, just before she put her hand on your shoulder. . . A whitish landscape. Completely deserted. I felt I was standing between high, yellow rocks on a mountain ridge and was looking over a desert which stretches to the horizon, a sea of stone and sand, with only an empty road winding through it. . .'

When I came to he was bending over me. The waitress held a chunk of ice to my neck. On the table I saw some blood between shards and spilled coffee.

'What happened?' I asked.

'You fainted.'

'How long?'

'Half a minute, a minute. How do you feel now?'

'A little better.'

While I said it I felt I had to throw up. Holding the hand of the waitress I ran to the restroom, sank on my knees, and vomited. Then I felt better. Gasping, I sat a little longer; the attendant opened the door slightly and said that I could wash myself. She showed me to a small room intended for changing babies. There was a hotplate for warming food and on a high commode lay a concave cushion of lightblue plastic. I felt quite a lot better, but in the mirror I looked like the ghost of my dead twin sister.

My forehead bled a little, and the attendant put a band-aid on it.

'I opened my eyes,' said the writer, 'and I saw you slowly double over just like the doll of a ventriloquist. Does this happen often?'

'It's just that I'm tired. I've been driving all day and I didn't sleep last night. I've been awake for more than thirty hours.'

'Except for just now. In any case, you're a reasonable woman, divorced from a critic too! Make a right turn to Avallon; take a hotel room and sleep. Or else I'll have your keys taken away by the Policia Stradale, or whatever you call that here in France. Imagine if this happens behind the wheel. You're a danger to yourself and humanity.'

I nodded, but he didn't quite believe me. He looked at his watch.

'Why don't you carry on to Amsterdam,' said I.

'You promise to do that?'

'Don't worry, I'll stay here for a while longer, and then I'll decide. You go and type your manuscript. If your front door does not open right away, it's because of all the newspapers piled up behind it.'

It started — not long after that afternoon in the museum —
with her not answering.

'Is something wrong, Sylvia?'

. . . .

'What are you staring at?'

. . . .

'Has something happened?'

She looked at me for a moment and then again into space.

. . . .

'Sylvia, for god's sake, say something!'

'There is nothing.'

'Are you getting your period?'

'No.'

'Then what is it?'

. . . .

'Don't you understand that you can't do that? You can't
close yourself off from me like that. What's happened to you
these last few days?'

. . . .

We had known each other almost half a year now. Some of
the flush of the early relationship had gone and in its place
new rules had evolved. She was young, she didn't know that
this quite normal; I wanted to help her to get through this
stage, explain it to her, tell her that something else came in
its place which instead of diminishing the relationship could
increase it — that in some sense our engagement was coming
to an end and the marriage beginning. But how could I do
that if she didn't let me near her?

'Is there something in our relationship that bothers you?'

. . . .

'Or are you bored? You want to do something? Let's talk about it. After all, you don't have to be a hairdresser if you don't feel like it. There are all kinds of jobs. I know enough people to help you get something interesting.'

. . . .

She developed a cleaning mania. Before we had vacuumed once a week at most, and then mostly for fun: it amused us to put on aprons, tie big red kerchiefs around our hair, open all the windows, and storm around like busy little housewives, a Frank Sinatra record on the phonograph. Now it would happen that she hadn't been for bread at noon because the bookcase in my study suddenly had to be cleaned. On a stepladder she stood wiping each shelf with a damp cloth and dusting each book separately.

'Why is that necessary, Sylvia?'

'Look at the dust. I'm sure it's never been done before.'

'Well, so what?'

'Dust is unhealthy, don't you know. Gives you allergies.'

'You?'

The next day the curtains had to be washed again and the windows rubbed with methyl. Or I noticed when I came home that the rugs were hanging over the balcony, and Sylvia had a rugbeater in her hand.

In bed however her initiative was on the decline.

'I'm tired, I have a bit of a headache.'

Sometimes I thought that she purposely used up so much energy in the daytime in order to be tired and headachy in the evening. Something wasn't right. Things were happening, some kind of process that somehow had to interrupted. Suddenly, while we were silently eating across from each other, I decided to put an end to it:

'Listen Sylvia, this isn't any good. Do you want to go home for a few days, to your mother?'

She nodded dully.

But she did not right away. Obviously she had thought

about it herself too, but didn't want to be the first to suggest it. Was I making a mistake, or was it the solution. I hoped that there in Petten she would look at the situation with different eyes.

It seemed to come as a relief to her. The rest of the evening we talked and fooled around with a mathematical game we had suddenly invented. We called it the World Giant. How long was the daily turd of the world giant? There were three thousand million people on earth, each producing an average turd of twenty centimeters; children a little shorter, in Europe and America a little longer than in the Third World, but altogether it came to about six hundred thousand kilometers, which is from here to the moon and back. We figured out the eye of the world giant and had to use the π r^2 formula, and I recall it was smaller than we had expected, something like the dome of a modest church, but possibly I had made an error.

'And now the prick,' said Sylvia. 'The hard prick of the world giant.'

When she wanted to start from scratch I pointed out it would be much faster if it could be deduced from the turd. First split it in half, because the women weren't involved, and then, using an average of ten centimeters, once again in half. Ten centimeters was of course on the short side, but we had to take little boys and old men into account. Nevertheless it reached from here halfway to the moon. We laughed and went to the window, but it was overcast.

'Are you sure you don't want to stay?' I said when we went to bed. 'We're doing alright aren't we?'

But she shook her head. Right away she sank into that sadness of hers. She turned her back to me, and I don't know if she quickly fell asleep. We said no more. I lay on my back staring in the dark, listening to her breathing. Melancholy covered me like a soft duvet.

When the alarm clock woke me the next morning she was still asleep. I got dressed, made tea and kissed her. Rightaway she put her arms around my neck, anguished.

'Are you leaving today?'

'I think it's better that way.'

'How long will you be gone?'

'I don't know, I don't know that, sweetheart.'

'Will you phone me in three days?'

'Yes.'

'Today is Tuesday, tomorrow Wednesday, day after tomorrow Thursday. Phone me Friday, after dinner.'

'Yes.'

'Promise?'

'Yes.'

When I came home at noon she was gone. The house was empty. I realized that I had hoped she would still be there, the table set, or even the place in a mess, and that she would fling her arms around me and say:- I didn't go, I don't know what was the matter with me but it's all gone, everything is alright again. But her toothbrush and things were gone from the bathroom. The bed was made; the two pillows on top of each other in the middle. In the kitchen the dishes were done and everything had been put away, — when I looked carefully I saw that she had even mopped the floor.

It was as if the house had been disinfected, like after an epidemic.

The next three days I spent primarily resisting the urge to phone her. It was like when I gave up smoking, and from the time of getting up to going to sleep I was involved with the non-lighting of a cigarette. 'It's simple as pie,' said Alfred, 'all you have to do is not light the next one.' That next cigarette became a thing which gradually dominated the whole world. Only by finally lighting it was the world liberated from that yoke.

The first evening I ate out in the city, but even during the fish soup I became uneasy with the idea that she might be calling. I bolted down the rest and rushed home. The rest of the evening I fought the desire to phone her to ask if perhaps she had been calling me. Maybe she was sitting at home hoping that I would call, and felt embarrassed to phone herself, so soon. But I didn't call, in case she felt pursued, when she had left especially to sort things out by herself.

When I came home the second night it seemed as if she had never been there. She didn't exist at all; I remembered her from some book or other that I had read somewhat too intensely. I was alone, a divorced woman with an older mother in Nice. But when I thought of my mother, she was suddenly real again. Because of her I was estranged from my mother, not through her fault, but through her existence. Since that afternoon in May I hadn't been in touch with her at all, and I hadn't heard from her either. How was she? Since then I had suppressed all thought about her, like someone who suppresses the thought of his income tax assessment – which works but only until the tax collector comes. I had to write her, right now, this was the moment. In my study I put a piece of paper in my typewriter, took it out again, and wrote by hand:

'Dear Mama!

It has been two months since we had that awful scene in Nice.'

I didn't get any further. I had no idea how to approach it. Besides which I could not concentrate. I fried two eggs and for the rest of the evening hung around, indecisive; for some reason it did not occur to me to turn on the TV. When I went to bed I left the door of the bedroom open so that I could hear the telephone.

Thursday night it was easier. There was a reception at the Rumanian Embassy in the Hague, and after that I went out for dinner with a few museum functionaries from Bucharest. I came home late and felt something like stage fright for the next evening.

On Friday while waiting for the telephone I tried to reconstruct for the umpteenth time what it really was in her that I felt so drawn to. I had been in love before, even with Alfred I had been in love, but with Sylvia it was something different, — and I don't believe it was because she was a woman. It could have just as easily been a boy. Or could it? I with a boy of twenty? I guess it really needed to be a women, if only not to be a gigolo, and if she had been as old as I, or older? Wasn't perhaps the fact that she was young the condition of it all? But then how about all the other young girls who left me cold?

At eight o'clock it suddenly occurred to me that she might not phone but come back instead. But perhaps she didn't have the key and the bell wasn't working. I ran down the stairs, opened the front door and pressed the bell. The bell worked. I pushed it again and imagined it was Sylvia.

But at eleven o'clock she still hadn't called. In a kind of stupor I sat there looking at the telephone, asking myself what I should do. 'After dinner' we had agreed, that is about eight o'clock, nine or nine-thirty at the most. What time does a superintendent's family in Petten eat? Probably about six! And what time do they go to bed? Surely not before twelve. While I waited I had the feeling that all the clocks on the earth had to pull themselves through time like so many little propellors.

At a quarter to twelve I couldn't stand it any longer: I was going to call her. I took the receiver from the hook and considered what I should say, but quickly put it down again in case she was just calling me. Right away I picked it up and dialed the number; I would see what happened; I no longer cared.

The change of the signal had a restful influence: already there was some kind of contact. It took a long time.

'Yes, hello?'

The voice of her father. I could hear that I had woken him up. Perhaps he thought there was trouble at the dyke.

'Mr. Nithart? This is Mrs. Boeken from Amsterdam.'

'Hello? What did you say?'

'This is Mrs. Boeken, Thomas' mother.'

'What time is it?'

'After eleven. Sorry if I disturbed you.'

'Is there something wrong with Sylvia?'

'I have a message for her, it might be urgent. Or is she asleep already?'

'Is Sylvia not with you?'

'What did you say?'

'Sylvia is not here, Sylvia is in Amsterdam.'

'Did she come back tonight?'

'Excuse me, has something happened? Please tell me right away.' By now he was wide awake.

'Not at all, please don't worry. I'm sure she'll be here soon. I'm sorry that I called you so late.'

'Sylvia was here briefly about three days ago. She left the same evening, like she always does.'

At the same moment I felt that my face had become rubber. A catastrophe had been in process during all those days. But before I could let that sink into my own mind, I first of all had to reassure her father and to end the conversation.

'Yes of course, I know Mr. Nithart. But this afternoon she said she had forgotten something in Petten, and then I thought she might have gone back for it. I imagine she'll be in the city at the moment with my son.'

'You scared me.'

'Please go back to sleep, there's nothing wrong.'

'Yes, while I'm speaking to you, Mrs. Boeken, is there any way we could get to meet Thomas? I understand we're not welcome in Amsterdam. Sylvia has always wanted to keep her life private, and she's always afraid that we will interfere. But it is only a normal interest on our part, after all she is our only child.'

I forced myself to speak quietly.

'I have told her so often, but I feel quite helpless about it.'

'When was it — Tuesday evening I asked her again, but right away she cut me off. Would it be possible for. . .' He didn't finish because I suddenly couldn't take it any longer.

'There's the doorbell,' I said. 'That'll be them. Goodnight Mr. Nithart, I'll do my best to advance your cause, and once again, sorry for calling you so late.'

'That's fine, that's fine. Goodnight then.'

I put the receiver down and started to shake. What was happening? She was going to go home for three days and then she would call me, but she had left the same day and hadn't called. She was somewhere, now, at this moment. Where was she? She was someplace where she didn't want to call me though she knew I was waiting for it. If an accident had happened I would have heard about it from her father. There was something else. I started to pace back and forth across the room as if I could find out where she was by thinking it through. Was it possible that she was gone for good? No, because all her clothes were still here.

Her clothes! I ran to the closet. The closet was empty.

Only hairpins, a torn panty, pieces of cotton batten, a broken brassière, and a coin of fifty centimes.

I dropped on the floor in front of the closet. She had taken everything, she would never come back. She had met someone, every day she had been alone and now she had finished the whole business and had run off with someone like the guy from the Zoo, some Thomas or other. Somebody had stolen my Sylvia! With open mouth I lay against the rug. 'Sylvia, dear Sylvia,' I sobbed, while my saliva, tears and snot made a wet spot under my face, and at the same time I saw myself in some strange way lying there on the floor, as if I had a separate eye stationed in a corner of the room near the ceiling.

The next day was Saturday. I didn't have to go to the museum. I still kept hoping that she would phone, but I didn't really believe she would. The house surrounded me, empty and dead. Wherever I walked I could see her. On the sofa, at the table, near the record player, near the window, in the kitchen, in the tub, in bed, in my study, dusting the books. The letter to my mother with one line on it went into the waste basket. I had chosen her over my mother; now I was just as alone as my mother. I put my hands on the seat of the easy chair where she used to sit with her knees drawn up. I didn't put my hands on myself although my own body had touched her most intimately of all. For me I did not exist, only she did. Somewhere she filled a space with her body, a small space, which she occupied, but I didn't know where that was.

'Will you phone me in three days?'

'Yes.'

'Promise?'

'Yes.'

I buttered a piece of bread and put it in my mouth, but I couldn't bite; my jaws stayed open and I put it down again. I went to sit on the sofa and again saw her back in front of the window of the jewelry shop, saw her again standing on the lawn in Nice.

'Sylvia isn't here, Sylvia is in Amsterdam.'

'Sylvia is in Amsterdam'

'Sylvia is not here, Sylvia is in Amsterdam.'

I groaned and dissolved into another extended crying fit. But while I cried, I remembered that one time when I had

cried just like this, when I was about seventeen — still in
Leiden. With a friend I had been to see a gangster film. It was
about a farmer's son who had come to the big city and ended
up in trouble. He had finally killed somebody, but was himself shot by the police. Mortally wounded he dragged himself
to his car and drove back to the country, on a long narrow
road with trees flashing by. I grabbed the arms of my chair, I
sat motionless while the trees shot by, left and right. When he
arrived at the farm of his parents he left the car with the
motor running, and stumbled bleeding into the pasture. In
the distance was a horse with its foal. When he fell dying in
the grass, the mare came running to him and pressed her
nozzle against his neck. THE END. The lights went on, and
sobbing I walked out of the cinema. But even on the street it
didn't stop, it became worse, my friend didn't know where
to hide himself he was so embarrassed. I walked into an alley
and with my face against a gutter pipe I wept and wept, not
realizing why.

I thought: if she saw me crying like this she might come
back. But she wasn't there to see it, it was as if I cried for
nothing. I washed my face and went out on the street.

'Will you come and live with me?'

'If that's what you want.'

'Sylvia is in Amsterdam.'

'Cross your feet.'

'She left the same evening, like she always does.'

I got dizzy, for a moment it was as if I were lifted half a
centimeter above the ground.

'I will always love you, you won't forget that?'

Of course that couldn't be, it had been an illusion. In the
afternoon while I was in the museum she had gone into the
city. In a boutique she had bought a blouse with the money
that was always in the top drawer, and she had gone to have a
cup of coffee in a student cafe.

'Let's get out of here. All these people. I want to be alone
with you, where we can talk in peace and quiet.'

'Alright!'
'Where shall we go'
'You decide.'
'Shall we go and have a drink at my house? I won't rape you.'
'Alright.'
'Alright.'
'Alright.'
'Shall we go and have a drink at my place? '
'Alright.'

I only thought of a man, a young man, the thought didn't enter my head that it could be a woman. I was the woman in her life, she in mine.

'Oh, so you are my mother?'
'Sylvia is not here.'
'You finally got me this far?'

I felt like a fly caught in midflight by someone with a folded newspaper and slapped into a corner. The whole day I drifted through the city, as if I were looking for her, although I didn't pay attention to what I was doing. In the afternoon I suddenly stopped and fished a piece of paper out of my purse that I had found once in the kitchen:

'bread
butter
coffee
eggs.'

As if that couldn't be remembered. It was written very thinly, with a pencil almost without pressure, very softly. It was the only writing I had by her. I looked at the round handwriting which showed that she had been taught a different letter style than my generation.

'The handwriting of betrayal,' I said out loud and put it away.

I hated her. That half-frigid creature that could only come after endless nonsense and then would suddenly pull her pelvis back, push me away and turn away troubled as if in pain.

Or was there no man at all? As soon as I thought that I turned in the direction of my house. Did she really just want to be by herself? The situation at home in Petten had bothered her and she went to stay with a girl friend. She had told her everything, from the beginning to the end, sitting on a straw mat, her legs under her body, in a little room with a Degas reproduction on the wall and a bamboo stand with plants. But why hadn't she phoned? Don't be silly, let her be for a while, her girlfriend had said. Or maybe she herself didn't feel comfortable and didn't want to hear my voice just yet. I would beg her to come back, but that wouldn't feel right at this point. Instead she had written me a long letter last night. I called a cab and went home. The evening delivery was at 5.30. When I paid the cabdriver I saw the mailman come out of the entrance. A sign! But in the mailbox I found only a card telling me that my driver's license would soon be expired and that for a small sum this could be renewed which would save me a lot of trouble. Perhaps he had put it in the wrong box. That sometimes did happen. I rang next door. From the loudspeaker near the bell came an electric female voice:

'Who is there?'

'The neighbour. Is there perhaps a letter from me in your box?'

The door buzzed open. The box was empty.

'Was there something?'

'You bet, I got it!' I called gaily.

'I guess from that nice young girl?'

'Yes,' I called and closed her door. 'Many thanks!'

On the entrance into my room I stood still. Everything unchanged. What in heaven's name was I going to do?

The phone rang. The sound was more beautiful than the trumpets of Jericho, — but it was Karin.

'Where on earth have you been all day?'

'Karin, I'm not in the mood.'

'What do you think I feel like?'

'What's the matter with you?'

'Oh, you haven't noticed? That sweet Sylvia of yours has run off with Alfred. But I am stuck with two children, you aren't.'

It was as it a disc had came flying from the depth of heaven and hit my forehead.

Tuesday night he had said that he had to go unexpectedly to Berlin for the Theaterwoche; actually he had gone into hiding with Sylvia in a hotel in Amsterdam. Only this afternoon he had gone over to tell Karin, afterwards he would come to see me. Sylvia and he had decided to stay together. Indignation was running high in Karin, but she didn't seem to be very sad. She gave me the address — somewhere near the Amstel.

'You had better go and see them,' she said.

Half crazy I got into my car and drove there. Hotel Hannie. An obscure place behind Rembrandsplein. In the hall hung the polished skin of a crocodile; at the back, a few steps lower, sat a fat man wearing only pants and an undershirt, smoking a cigar, the room stuffed with furniture and knick knacks, everything in red and beige and made of cut glass: the boudoir of a German film about the Mayerling drama, viewed through the wrong end of binoculars.

'I'm looking for Mr. Boeken.'

'Room one,' he wheezed.'

That was at the front. I knocked hard and immediately opened the door. Alfred was reading on the double bed. I looked around the doll-sized room.

'Where is Sylvia?'

Quickly he put his book away, and swung his legs onto the floor.

'Listen . . .'

'Where is Sylvia, goddammit!' I screamed. He came over to me.

'Don't touch me! Where is Sylvia?'

I saw in his eyes what I looked like, that he was afraid I

would do something to her. He went to the circular staircase
which ended in the corner of the room.

'Sylvia?' he said.

Through the narrow opening Sylvia came out of the basement — first her pale face and her narrow shoulders, next the
black dress which she had worn at the theatre. When I saw it,
her here, with Alfred, not with me, it was as if somewhere
deep in my body I felt something change, that somehow
something down there had shifted and became irrevocably
warped.

Without saying anything I embraced her and pressed my
face into her neck. She let it happen, but her arms hung
beside her body, everything inert. When I noticed that I let
her go immediately. It was definitely finished. I wanted to
leave right away, but when I saw how anguished her face had
become I couldn't go.

'Leave us alone for a minute,' I said to Alfred, and when
he hesitated: 'Get the hell out of here! I won't murder her!'

He disappeared down the stairwell and I sat down on the
edge of the bed.

'Sit down,' I said.

She shook her head.

'What is happening, Sylvia? What are you doing in this
whore-house?'

She said nothing.

'Is this it? Is it finished between us?'

'Better not talk any more,' she said and stood before me
like a girl that's been called before the matron.

I felt she wouldn't say anything else. Should I grab her and
drag her violently into my car and take her home? And then?
Lock her up? She was a meter away from me and it was as if
I felt the warmth of her body. I couldn't leave. It was like
someone who, on the last day of his holidays has packed his
suitcase, called the taxi, and sits down in the sun for another
minute, eyes closed.

'You'd better go,' I said. 'Better call Alfred.' I covered my face with my hands because I didn't want to see her disappear through the hole. 'Goodbye, Sylvia.'

What looks did they exchange downstairs? Did they quickly kiss each other? Did they press each other's hand?

Alfred came upstairs and sat down on a chair beside the sink.

'This afternoon I came to your door to tell you, but you weren't there.'

I lifted my face and looked at him.

'Alfred have you gone completely mad?' He lowered his eyes. 'How long has this been going on?'

'You know that.'

'Did you make a date that night on the balcony?'

'No, I phoned her the next afternoon.'

'So you initiated it?'

'If you like. But if it had come from my side only I wouldn't have dared to phone her, you must realize that.'

'And then you saw each other every day after that?'

'Regularly.'

'And then you went regularly to bed with each other.'

'No. That only happened here.'

'And last Tuesday? Did Sylvia phone you and say that she was leaving me for a few days.'

'Yes.'

I thought I was going to throw up in my misery.

'And then you came here to try it out for a while. Is that why it took so long?'

'Yes — but not the way you mean.'

'Oh, you mean more spiritually. Yes, I'm sure, and if it didn't work out then you would simply have been in Berlin, and Sylvia with her parents, and Karin and I would never have noticed anything.'

'But it did work out.'

I nodded.

'And now you are Thomas.'

'Thomas? What do you mean?'

'Oh, you don't know yet?' I couldn't help it, my eyes suddenly filled with tears. 'Why in god's name is it her, Alfred? Because I was with her?'

'No. Because of herself.'

'And Karin? and the children you needed so badly? Do you really know what you've started?'

'Yes,' he said, 'I know that exactly. I'll stay with her. I don't intend to divorce Karin, but if Sylvia wants it I will get a divorce.'

To hear him use her name that way was almost harder to bear than seeing her in the same room with him.

'And does she want that?'

'It has not been discussed.'

So that's how it was. I said nothing. I had to leave, but the presence of Sylvia, right under me, kept me there.

'You know,' said Alfred, 'every person has the feeling I think, that he really does not belong to the life of other people. That in some way or other he is different, a guest, and he makes all possible effort to make sure that the others won't notice. That is the feeling which all people share, and that's exactly why they belong together. But with Sylvia I too have the feeling that she does not belong, that she is something different, that she really does not exist. That's why in some strange way she decreases that feeling in myself, because I have to make her belong. I think that's how it is, and then the only thing I can say is that after you she has chosen me in order to exist.'

I stood up and walked out of the door, without a word.

I left the car and started to walk along the Amstel. When I came to the fence of a demolished house I sat on the steps to the basement which were still intact. With my eyes on the boarded-up door and the rotting remnants which overflowed from the torn garbage bags, I thought of what he had said. He had carefully put into words what I had always felt. With all her sagacity she didn't really exist, — her sagacity was supposed to fill that void. Did she belong more to him than to me because he was able to articulate it and I couldn't?

There was only one person who could have answered that, but he was dead.

In the afternoon in the neighbourhood of Lyon a large black sports car passed me. Though I was doing a hundred and thirty kilometres it passed me so fast that I might have been standing still. A man and a woman were in it. I suddenly had a glimpse of the hotel where they were going: the white palace in Cannes, or in Monte Carlo, with the high wrought iron gate and the finely gravelled driveways.

With a leap it disappeared over the hill, and it seemed as if its image had for a moment stayed there, suspended.

'Where are you?'

Never was his presence so strong in his study as when he was not there. Against my mother's wishes, as a young girl I often sneaked into it when he was lecturing. The books. The long oak table with papers. The armchair in front of his desk. the worn out leather easy chair for the students in which I saw Alfred for the first time when I came in to bring tea. All those cupboards, and tables and shelves. A man's study has to be crammed with things, or be aesthetically empty, — something in between, like Alfred's room later on, is never right. Without touching anything I would stand still for a while, and then it was as if I were in his body.

'Are you in papa's room again?'

It was February and the sun shone warmly through the glass and the garden. Spring! I ran outside, but there was a freezing cold wind. Quickly I went inside again, behind the glass doors. Only then did I see the rippling, black rain puddles in the grass.

'You know that I don't want you going in there.'

Three quarters of an hour later my backview mirror

showed a car just like before. It gained on me as fast as before, or faster, as if it was chasing the first one. They had stopped somewhere for something to eat or drink.

But twenty minutes later I ended up in a line of cars. After five minutes I saw the red and blue flashing lights. down the road. Police directed us to the left lane where we slowly filed by them. Across on the shoulder stood a car transporter with a semitrailer double-deckered with new cars. There they had crawled under, as if they were afraid of something. For a second I could see them both sitting in their torn-open automobile: forward, in sleep, while the giant engine filled them from lap to chin: they had caught up with themselves.

A stone was growing inside my body, a large boulder, the kind you don't find in Holland and which some people put in the trunk of their car when abroad to bring home for the garden.

In the morning, on the way to work, it seemed as if the whole city was infected. They were both in the city, as likely still asleep, she on her back and with her arms above her head showing the hair in the armpits which I wouldn't let her shave because I consider its an anti-sexual ladies' custom; he with an arm around her waist and a leg across her thighs. Because of them the streets looked to me the way they did in wartime photographs. When I got to the museum and saw that Mr. Roebljov was not yet at his table, I quickly turned the guestbook back to her signature: she had written her name no differently than the way she wrote bread or salt. Her love declaration of that afternoon had been a farewell speech. She had already met him by then and in that disgusting hotel of course. Once everyone knew about them, they moved on to the Hotel Krasnapolsky on the Dam, as Karin had told me. Now and then Karin called me. I couldn't muster the strength to look her up and to sit with her as some distorted mirror image of Sylvia and Alfred. Every time she asked what was happening now. I believe she felt that it was my responsiblity to get things back to normal. I was to blame for everything: first I had given Alfed to her, who had then deserted her, and for someone who again came from me. I was really supposed to move in with her and be a father for her children, then the circle would be complete.

I didn't visit my former friends and acquaintances. When I

ran into them and allowed them to see a glimmer of my
despair, their lukewarm response implied that they really
couldn't be bothered. Marriages, separations, they happened
in their world too, but you didn't make a big scene, that was
old-fashioned and immature, — and when it concerned a
woman or girl, then that was completely ridiculous. It was as
if they wanted to say: — Be a big boy.

But I wasn't a big boy — any more than the other big boys.
Sometimes at night I couldn't control myself and before I
went to sleep I would drive by the Krasnapolsky. Once I had
already passed it when I saw them coming around the corner
along the dark canal. He had his arm around her shoulders. I
don't know if I thought of accelerating, jumping the curb and
running them down at that moment, or if it is only coming to
me now. Anyhow, I didn't and instead turned the headlights
on bright because I didn't want them to recognize the car.
Alfred put his arm before his face, but Sylvia never even
closed her eyes: she looked straight into the high beam.

Everything I did those weeks in July was accompanied by
the uninterrupted realization that she was no longer with me.
I did as little as possible, I preferred to just sit in my room
looking at nothing. Or I would look at the photo in the
reptile house where we stood with arms linked and smiling,
taken by Thomas. I sat in the slow passage of time as someone waiting for something which he knows can take a long
time. I've always felt that way in airplanes. I was never really
afraid of falling, but there was always some kind of awareness
so that I had to constantly pay attention to the flight; if I let
that go and started to read something, even if it was only the
directions for the emergency life jacket under my chair, the
engines would immediately take advantage of that and
develop all kinds of mechanical defects and finally no doubt
they would stop or catch on fire. So for the entire journey I
look at the passing landscape down below, or into the
blinding white of the clouds against the window in which the
aircraft seems to stand still, or even fly backward.

I read one book: the letters of Abelard and Heloïse. I didn't know I owned it. It had shown up when Sylvia was cleaning the closets. It was a collector's edition; on the inside of the front cover was my father's signature dated before my birth.

The first letter was directed to a friend who was in trouble: 'I have decided to write you the story of my misfortunes by way of consolation.' When in 1118 he met and tempted Heloïse he was already one of the most famous philosophers of his time; from his school, which he had established on a hill outside the Paris of those days, the Sorbonne was born. Heloïse was seventeen, twenty-two years younger than he. She lived with the canon Fulbert who called himself her uncle but who was probably her natural father, — at least mine had pencilled that in the margin. When she became pregnant, he kidnapped her and she delivered a child which they named Astrolabius. Fulbert, who loved his daughter madly, was beyond reason. Against the desire of Heloïse, who was opposed to a marriage and would rather remain his mistress, Abelard finally agreed with him that he would marry her, but in secret, otherwise it would endanger his theological career. 'Just like Fulbert himself it seems,' said the pencilled margin. But Fulbert made sure it became public knowledge after all, upon which Heloïse swore that it was untrue and moved to a convent to end the rumours. But then Fulbert suspected that Abelard had forced her to this and responded as follows: 'On a night, while I slept, they avenged themselves with a terrible and degrading punishment which shook the world in amazement. They robbed me of those parts of my body which performed the act which they so deplored.'

I had the feeling that I myself was the friend to whom he wrote. But it didn't comfort me, because at the same time I myself felt like the poor castrated Pierre who meanwhile had entered a monastery. Heloïse was shown the letter, and she in turn wrote him that their love must unite them again, if need be at the cost of eternal damnation. 'I crave the error of my ways, I thirst after it. I relive those things with you and even in sleep I cannot rest. Sometimes an unconscious move of my body betrays the thoughts which are ever present.'

That was in the night, in the night I was Heloïse.Abelard referred her to God, and their letter exchange ended in theological jargon, – in my case it was nature. Perhaps it was because I wasn't eating enough, but sometimes it was as if Sylvia communicated through the entire world. One evening an overwhelming sunset poured itself over Leidesplein and the theatre, such as I had never seen before in the city. Buildings and traffic were elevated to a breathless existence endlessly changing in a fairylike process. Small skylights transmitted orange signals, tramrails turned to gold. I stood between it and no longer moved. Sylvia, I thought, Sylvia. I stood still until everything ended up in a soft violet and then suddenly slid back into the clear grey from which it had emerged.

At the end of July I came home from the museum and found in the letterbox a small piece of paper which had been torn from a calendar:

'I'll be coming by at around at eight o'clock to talk to you about something. — Sylvia.'

For a full minute I stood there looking at it. That handwriting. She had been here. My first impulse was to phone her, but then she might say over the phone what she wanted to discuss, and I wouldn't see her. But if it was something that could be said by telephone she would have called me instead. It was something else, something she had to see me about personally. It was something important.

Did she want to come back?

Had it all been a prank? A little adventure which she tired of after a few weeks? I was completely unprepared for this possibility. Would she want to go and get her things later, if it was alright with me? At what cost? I read the note again and again. It was impersonal, no salutation, not even my name. She wanted to 'talk to me': did that refer to something serious? Perhaps she was unsure of my reaction, and wanted to give me no chance to guard myself in advance. On the other hand, if she really wanted to come back, she could have simply come; she still had the key.

I didn't know. But to be on the safe side I went out and bought a bottle of champagne. When I put it in the refrigerator I suddenly felt full of energy. It was six o'clock and I wished she had written that she could not come till ten. It was a warm summer evening. I opened the windows and started to clean up my papers which had not been done in

weeks, leafed through books and turned on the television.
Even the assurance that she would be here soon, for whatever
reason, gave a horizon to my existence — like an astronaut
who returns from outer space to the atmosphere.

While I was watching the news, the bell rang. I pulled the
cord to open the door and saw her at the bottom of the stairs
— a stream of warm air came up the stairs, at the same time
as her image, passed me and left the house via the room
through the windows.

'May I come up?'

In the room she looked around in a way which showed
that many other impressions had already been superimposed
on her memory. She looked around the way I always do
when I come back from a trip abroad: everything seems
familiar, but somehow compressed, too familiar. She did not
look well. Around her neck she wore a small green scarab on
a golden chain. I took it in my hand.

'From Alfred?'

'Yes.'

On her finger she still wore our ring, the way I did.

'Do you want something to drink?'

She shook her head.

'I'm not staying long.'

She sat down and started to roll a cigarette. The nails of
her right hand had disappeared again.

'How are you, Sylvia?'

'Alright,' she said and looked at me, 'and you?'

I shrugged.

'Awful. But you already knew that.'

She nodded and pulled her tongue along the paper.

'You're getting skinny,' she said.

'As if I were ever fat. But you, why do you look so awful
if you're alright?'

After a few seconds she looked at me again.

'I've come to get my passport.'

The champagne would stay in the refrigerator.

'Your passport?' I stared at her. At the same moment I remembered that it was still with mine; when we went to Nice she had put it with mine. She had forgotten to take it with her, and all this time it had been the only thing of hers I still had.

'Why?'

'I'm going to London.'

'With Alfred?'

'Yes.'

'For how long?'

'I don't know. He doesn't want to stay in Amsterdam. He can become a theatre reporter or something. He's also writing a book.'

Finally he was writing his Book, which he'd always been bugging me about, — Sylvia was his muse.

'And your parents? What do they know about all this?'

'My parents don't have anything to do with him. They think Thomas received a scholarship to Oxford.'

'Oxford. Did Alfred suggest that?'

'Yes.'

Of course, I thought, Oxford, — the jerk.

'And if your mother comes by here I suppose you want me to keep on playing that game, for your convenience?'

'If you like. Or else you'd look awfully silly yourself.'

That was quite true.

'Yet I don't understand it,' I said. 'In our case it was a fairytale necessary for my sake because they weren't supposed to know you lived with a woman. But couldn't you have simply told them that it was finished between you and Thomas and that you're now with my divorced husband? With Thomas' father then, such things do happen, just as in the reverse.'

'As long as I understand it.'

'Why Alfred is willing carry on this nonsense I can't understand either. He wants to go on living with you? Then why does he build his new life on a lie?'

'Because I want it.'

'And why do you want it?'

She was silent. She wasn't going to say it. After a while I asked:

'When are you going?'

'As soon as I have passport.'

'You won't get it.' I said.

'Then I'd better go.'

I remained seated and crossed my legs.

'You talked about that, right? If I didn't give to to you, you would leave right away and apply for a new passport tomorrow at the townhall in Petten. That would only make a few days' difference.'

'Yes.'

'And you know as well that you could submit a complaint against me with the police?'

'Yes, but we didn't want to do that.'

'How kind of you. I suppose he is waiting for you outside in the car?'

'No.'

'Wasn't he afraid that I would hurt you or something?'

When she didn't answer I went to my desk and found her passport. I opened it to look at her photo: a much younger girl. It looked more like the girl I had met half a year ago than the one standing now in my room. I suddenly saw how she had changed: something round and downy had gone from her face, it had become harder, more like a woman.

I gave her the passport. We said no more. Before she went down the stairs, her hand already on the handrail, she looked at me for a moment with an incomprehensible, beaming expression on her face.

Somewhere near Orange, where the first cypresses began to dot the landscape, I caught myself dreaming now and then — or rather, they were scenes which appeared briefly while I was driving. I thought of the hairfine little jets which I once saw spouting up from Sylvia. I had stroked her, and suddenly from her genitals sprang a webfine, clear little fountain, so beautiful and artistic that I spent several hours in vain the next day looking for such a fountain in the art records. I knew I had seen it somewhere, and now I suddenly remembered where: In the drawing DIE TAGESZEITEN by Runge, a Romantic German painter of around 1800. The step from there to the plumed Roman grotesques in the Engelenburcht was suddenly obvious to me.

At that moment I saw my father and mother above the road, arm in arm and in white; in the distance stood a white horse.

I thought about where I had, in reality, earlier seen such little fountains. With Karin. She had had her first child, the young father estatically happy had phoned me and like a good sport I had gone over to admire mother and baby. When the child had been put back in the cradle she showed me one of her breasts: in its depths the tissue had burst and looked like marble. At that moment the child began to cry, and almost sooner than her ears could have heard it, the milk spouted from her nipple in just such small jets.

Then I suddenly saw a street I didn't recognize, late in the evening, there were great mansions and giant trees, it stormed and three little girls were blown helplessly down the lane by the storm, enveloped in yellow clouds of autumn leaves, their legs spread, their feet away from the madly racing pedals and their hair blowing ahead of them, their eyes large with fear, wondering where they would end up.

And another time I had seen them was when a turkey's throat was cut. I was still quite small and during the Christmas holidays I was at Henny Hoenderdos' farm for a few days. In the bare branches of a tree hung a kind of spongy, transparent cushion: the afterbirth of a foal. He and his sister had to hold down a turkey with both their arms — his father pulled the head up and with a short, broad knife he cut thoughtfully through the neck, just like you cut a thick rope. Jets sprang from there too, but much higher than the other two times, a fountain of blood.

At that moment I saw a dark deserted grassy field in the late dusk: rectangular, surrounded on three sides by woods which had already turned black. It seemed that it was sending out a message, but I could not decode it.

And then it happened.

I drove on the road, as I had been doing for hours, — and suddenly something snapped and I stood still, while at the same moment the road which was under me was being pulled towards me with a speed of a hundred and thirty kilometers per hour. Frightened I grabbed the steering wheel, my eyes on the road speeding under me. I started to but I couldn't take my eyes off the road to look in the rearview mirror. Carefully I decreased speed, that is the speed of the road, and steered the shoulder toward me, while I was passed by angrily honking drivers.

The earth stood still. I turned the flashing lights on and turned the engine off. Right away the heat and the silence came in. What was the matter? I was tired, I had skipped a night's sleep and had driven the whole day, but I had never heard of this kind of thing. I looked outside. The cypresses stood like black candleflames in the early dusk; the moon was hanging above the Provençale landscape.

I couldn't stay here. I turned the starter, accelerated carefully, and slowly the earth under me resumed its motion. I kept the flashing lights on and made sure the shoulder stayed under me; I kept its speed below fifty. After about ten minutes I started to get used to it and increased speed a little, but immediately I became dizzy.

AVIGNON – *Nord*

It was clear that I would never get to Nice this way. I would take a room in Avignon, have a good sleep and then tomorrow I would feel better. Why had I not listened to the playwright?

Near the Péage was one green light. Cautiously, I pulled it towards me and manoeuvered the narrow entrance around me. A moment later the wall of the city slid by on my left side and the Rhone on my right; the water was alive; great, leafed branches were being carried along; here and there the water flowed in glistening little eddies against its own current. On the opposite side the foliage of the dark trees hung down in the river. When the half-bridge approached, the city wall changed to rock; there were holes in it with little lamps, and I could hear loud pop music coming out. I can't say that I followed the signs to the tourist information – I was still on the same moving universe where it had first happened to me. In the interior of the earth there was an incredibly complicated, universal machinery which was connected to my steering wheel and my accelleration pedal.

Slowly the gate slid toward me and the city folded itself around me. It was busy in the narrow streets with the stores still open, and now I also had to take into account the independant movement of people who crossed the moving street. When I saw an open space at the sidewalk I somehow managed to get it under my car. I decided to take my suitcase and walk the rest of the way. But when I had locked the car and started to walk around it, I immediately had to grab hold of it: I wasn't walking; instead with my feet I had brought the earth into motion; the whole city revolved around me. Driving seemed to be easier. I pulled the car on again like an iron coat, and after fifteen minutes or so I ended up at the station square, near the tourist bureau.

'Aren't you feeling well?' asked the lady behind the counter, worried. I had to hold on to anything I could get hold of, like someone on the ice. 'Shall I phone a doctor?'

'Please don't go to any trouble, it'll go away.'

'Are you sure?'

'It's only exhaustion.'

'Exhaustion?' She looked as it she didn't believe me.

'I've had it before, it's nothing.' I sat down. 'I'm looking for a room for the night.'

'A room, a room, easily said, everything is full as far as Tarasçon. It's the tourist season, and there are two conventions in the city. A room. . .' she said and thought about it. 'Of course, you must have a room. Do you mind a room in a private home?'

'Anything will be fine.'

She looked at me hard, and then decisively picked up the phone. While she was explaining the situation to someone, I looked out onto the busy street. I couldn't imagine that something was wrong with me and that I would notice it as soon as I moved.

'Fine. Bye mother, I'll call you later.' She put the receiver down. 'It's with my mother, on the Place du Palais. As far as the price is concerned. . .'

'That makes no difference to me. I am very grateful to you. Do you think I can leave my car here and take a cab?'

'Impossible.'

'I would rather not drive again.'

'One moment.' She opened a door and asked a man if he would drive me somewhere in my car, saying he could go straight home after that, and to me she said: 'We're closing soon anyway.'

After she had asked me again if I really didn't want a doctor, a tall man appeared who could not have been very old, but already had a grey beard. He gave me his arm, so that I could avoid all approaching obstacles easily. Now and then he said something in a dialect which I found hard to understand; he managed the long busy street with the greatest of ease, navigated a square which was filled with dining people, avoided carefully the sides of a narrow entrance after which we had to stop near the bottomless pit.

Supporting me with his arm, holding my suitcase in his other hand, he led me to my new address. He rang the bell and said that he would park the car on the other side of the hole; he would throw the keys in the mailbox. Then the door was opened by an old lady, completely in black.

A few days after Sylvia's departure for England I started another letter to my mother.

'Dear Mama!

It is of course unforgivable that I have not written you after what happened in May. But in the meantime so many other things have happened. To begin with I want to ask your forgiveness for the lies I used when I tried to protect you from the truth. Rightly or wrongly I wanted to protect you, but right away you knew that something wasn't right, and then everything was wrecked by the person I was trying to hide from you. Recently our relationship has ended, that's why I can talk about it now.'

Did I have to tell her that she was now with Alfred, her former son-in-law? Could I ask that of her, or did I have to protect her again, keep things from her and twist the facts.

Again this letter wasn't getting anywhere.

I used the rest of the paper and the back to change my signature. I've had an urge to do that for the past several weeks. Of course it has changed some over the years, but not significantly. As a girl I had changed it radically at least three times; the last variation I had kept and it had developed to a speedy arabesque in the form of a flying bird. Now I suddenly had a need for something legible, more formal if necessary. Of course I would have to keep up my old one as well because it was registered with the bank, was on the I.D. card of my pay cheques and in my passport.

I also went to the hairdresser and had my hair cut short.

'Madam, it is of course your decision, but are you sure you want me to do this?'

'I'm perfectly sure.'

'You realize that it will probably never grow this long again?'

'I know that.'

'I must honestly tell you that I really hate to do this. This is the work of a lifetime. We get ladies here who would give anything to have hair like this.'

'Then why don't you sell it to them?'

'Don't you want a wig made out of it?'

'I don't want to see it again, it has to go, and immediately.'

'As you wish. It is done in a second. But to be on the safe side I'll keep it for a few weeks.'

Next I went to the doctor.

I had always been skinny, but now I had lost another five kilos, and the dizzy spells had started to bother me. In the morning when I got out of bed I sometimes keeled right over against the closet. The doctor had diagnosed it quickly: blood-pressure too high. He sent me to a heart specialist who made x-rays and a cardiogram, and then told me to pick up a large bottle and a bag of salt at the hospital. I had to eat that and for twenty four hours I had to urinate only in the bottle. Then I had to eat more salt and not drink anything: When I had emptied myself completely, I went to the hospital where they shoved me in a machine as large as a room. But my kidneys appeared to be alright too: essentially it was hypertension.

'Be pleased that we have caught you, Madam. With a salt-free diet and some tablets we'll get it down quite easily.'

'How do you get something like that?'

He turned up his palms in resignation.

'Nobody knows.'

Among hundreds of young people on a Saturday afternoon I then went to sit on the steps of the monument of the Dam — opposite Krasnapolsky where they had lived. I asked myself what to do with the rest of my life. Sylvia was in London and walked on tiptoes because her lover was writing a book about the influence of theatre conventions on the theatre; in the evening she went with him to the theatre and at night she went to bed with him. I could do one of two things: remain celibate the rest of my life and build churches in places where she had ever stood or sat — or deliberately dismiss her from my existence, live my life and remember her as an unforgettable performance I had been allowed to be part of. I already knew that I would choose the latter, perhaps had already chosen, — that I had let myself go very far until finally ending up in repulsive, ochre-coloured machines, but that the experience had in effect reached the hard core of my soft being. As far as that was concerned I was a peach.

It had lasted not quite half a year: in February we had been standing beside each other looking at the golden owl, now it was August. I could see that period before me in a three dimensional way, as I always saw a year in three dimensions. It is a large figure in the shape of an egg, about seventy meters long and forty wide at its widest. In the course of the year I move slowly along that line, following the hands of the clock. The months cover uneven segments: almost the entire round bottom is occupied by December, just past the pointed end is August. From January I look constantly in the direction of the top, but comes August I suddenly turn and look in the direction of December. This was not only this year, it is that way every year. Now that I write it down I suddenly realize that I never talked about it to anyone. Perhaps it is strange and others may not even understand what I'm talking about.

When Henny Hoenderdos had walked away past the palace, I was so irritated that I had to pee. I walked into the Krasnapolsky and arrows sent me down into the basement. There I sat in a small cubicle, where the heat was incredible. Behind the walls it hummed, apparently because the central heating system was being checked; a big, vertical pipe was burning hot; high up was a small window which probably opened out into an alleyway. While I emptied myself out in that heat I felt so comfortable that it was like being back inside my mother.

Slowly I started to feel a bit more at home in the world. In the morning I read the paper and looked in the entertainment column at what was happening in the city. Not that I went anywhere, but I did walk into a bookstore occasionally at noon. In a shop in the Spiegelstraat I found myself interested in an illustrated volume of Gustave Moreau and I bought it.

At night near the open window I read the introduction. They cited Huysmans who in his novel A REBOURS had written of the Salome of Moreau: 'She is more or less naked. In the dizziness of the dance her veils have come undone, the brocade has slid to the ground and only precious, wrought metals and transparent jewels covered her body. As a great lock a magnificent jewel flashes and sparkles in the cleavage between her breasts.' Those were the words Oscar Wilde would recite to himself in jail when he could not sleep: 'As a great lock a magnificent jewel flashes and sparkles in the cleavage between her breasts. . .' Why? I remember putting down the book and leaning out of the window. What was the matter with that sentence? It surely wouldn't be women to whom Wilde's thoughts turned when he could not sleep. Suddenly I knew it. Those breasts with the cleavage were a boy's buttocks, and the flashing jewel between then was the anus. It was the cunt of Lord Douglas!

I recall that I laughed — and while I was laughing I saw a taxi stopping in front of the house and Sylvia getting out. Right away she looked up and waved enthusiastically, with both arms.

'Sylvia!' I yelled.

'Laura!'

At the same moment I was drunk. I reeled through the room and down the stairs. 'O God,' I said. 'O God. O God.' I coughed because I had screamed at the top of my voice.

Outside she flew right away into my arms and kissed me and started to jump around with me.

'Sylvia, Sylvia, what is this?' I had become hoarse, I could only whisper.

The cabdriver put a large suitcase and a bag on the steps; with an elbow on the roof of his car he assumed a pose of endless patience.

'That I'm going to tell you,' said Sylvia and she settled the bill with him. She wore a wide, white cotton dress almost to the ground. With the suitcase I followed her up the stairs. I no longer knew my way round my little world. But I managed to bring her suitcase up the stairs. There were bare feet in the place! Nothing of anything that was happening could I understand at this point. Was it really happening?

In the room she turned around, spread her arms and said:

'I am pregnant.'

I froze.

'I am pregnant,' she said again. 'That is what you wanted, didn't you? You wanted a child from me?' She laid her hands on her stomach. 'I've come to bring it to you.'

I stood a little longer and then I gave up. I walked to her and with her I fell on the sofa. I don't know how long I lay there, staring with wide open eyes into the pillow to let it sink in.

'You've cut your hair,' said Sylvia finally. 'Did you save it?'

I sat up a little.

'From Alfred?'

'From you.' She kissed me. 'Via Alfred.'

I took her face in my hands.

'Was that your intention from the beginning, Sylvia?'

'Of course,' she said in a tone of 'how could I ever have thought anything different.'

'Then why didn't you tell me?'

'As if you would have let me. Why are you whispering all the time?'

I looked into her eyes, into that innocent, cruel secret.

'I have to drink something,' I said and stood up.

In the kitchen I took the bottle of champagne from the icebox and stood there with it in my hands. It was as if my brain wouldn't work any more. Everything that had happened had meant something different: it hadn't happened, something else had happened. It had all been for me. My agony was the price I had to pay for the child that I wanted, the substitute for the birthpains, the contractions, the tearing.

'You shouldn't leave the icebox open.' She closed the door and put her arms around my neck. 'Are you glad?'

She asked me as if she had given me a bracelet or a nice book.

'Yes,' I said.

'I won't ever leave again.'

'Yes,' I said again. 'Of course I am happy. It's just that I can't . . .'

'Better give me that bottle.'

When I walked into the room with the glasses she had pulled up her dress and taken the bottle between her knees. The cork hit the ceiling and a thick jet foamed up between her legs. Quickly I held the glasses under it.

'To our child.' She held up her glass and we toasted. After she had taken a big swallow she said: 'I hope it will be a boy. And you?'

'Either is fine.'

'Why are you crying?'

'Am I crying?' I felt my cheek, it was wet with tears. 'Yes,' I said, 'I'm crying.'

'You shouldn't cry. What's there to cry about?'

'It's because I still can't comprehend it all.'

Sylvia put down her glass.

'I'll go and unpack,' she said and knelt beside her suitcase. For her the business was finished.

'Just a minute, you have to tell me some more.'

'About what?'

'Does Alfred know about this?'

'I left a note for him.'

'A note? How do you mean?'

'He had to be told about it!'

'Yes, but . . . Did you just come from London?'

'Of course. Three days ago I thought I was pregnant and I went to have a check-up. This morning I received the verdict: I was. So right away I packed my suitcase and left a note for Alfred which told him all about it, and that I was going back to you. He was at the library of the British Museum.'

'So when he came home this afternoon. . .'

'He would have found my note of course.'

I put my glass down and took her hands in mine.

'Sylvia,' I said, 'this is simply not possible.'

'What isn't?

'That you have a child by him and you leave a note.'

'Why not? I'm not married to him! I haven't been using the pill for half a year. I didn't write that I was having a child by him, only that I was pregnant. I can always say that I went to bed with all kinds of people while he was working in London. That child isn't his at all, that child is yours. If it's a boy we'll call him Thomas.'

'We must call him,' I said. 'The three of us have to talk about this.'

Full of indignation she looked at me.

'Why are you defending him like that? He hasn't been that great to you.'

'He left his wife and children for you, Sylvia.'

'That's his business, I didn't force him.'

I was worried and uncertain. It was almost inhuman what she was doing.

'I almost wish you hadn't written anything,' I said. 'After

nine months he would have been back with Karin and laughing at me because you walked around with a big stomach.'

At that moment the phone rang.

'That's him,' said Sylvia. 'Don't answer.'

'Of course I have to answer. The sooner this is settled the better.

'Hello?'

'Laura? Is that you?'

'Yes.'

'This is Alfred. Is Sylvia with you?'

'Yes.' During the entire conversation I didn't take my eyes off Sylvia.

'Did she tell you?'

'Yes.'

'I can hardly understand you, your voice is so soft. Listen carefully. I'm alright. But we have to talk about this.'

'I agree.'

'I've been thinking a long time before calling. If she really wants to be back with you in the condition she is in now, then I can understand that, but I have to talk about it. After all it is my child.'

'According to Sylvia that isn't certain,' I said.

He was silent for a moment.

'Oh. I want to sleep on it first and then I'll come to Amsterdam tomorrow morning.'

'About what time?'

'I've already reserved a seat for the 9 o'clock flight. Then I'll be at your house about eleven or eleven-thirty.'

'Alright.'

'But I want to speak to her alone, if that's alright. You have to understand that.'

'I understood it before you did, Alfred.'

'And please don't tell Karin about any of this yet.'

'No. Do you want to speak to Sylvia?'

Sylvia looked up from the book of Moreau which she had found on the table and shook her head emphatically.

'Tomorrow. Just go to work. When you come home at
noon the three of us can talk for a bit and then I'll leave. I
won't bother you. I've already resigned myself. I know what
kind of woman she is. See you tomorrow.'

'Till tomorrow.' I put the phone down. 'He's coming here
tomorrow at 11.'

Sylvia shrugged her shoulders and closed the book with a
hard slap.

'You have to do it for me,' I said hoarsely.

The whole evening I kept on whispering. When the
champagne was finished we went out for dinner. I was
relieved that it would be settled so quickly with Alfred. I suspected that he might actually be pleased with this develop-
ment; after only a few hours he had accepted it, which was
rather soon. He had probably been longing for his two small
sons and his wife, – especially now that he was busy with his
book. I knew him pretty well. He was a person who had to be
able to discuss intellectual matters. He could do that with
me, with my half-completed art history study, and Karin had
studied law, but Sylvia didn't even know the difference
between Sophocles and Beckett, since she doesn't know who
either Sophocles or Beckett is. It didn't bother me that she
didn't know that, I knew the most unpleasant people who
did know. I loved her because of who she was.

'This is just like a restaurant in London where I sometimes
went with Alfred,' she said excitedly when we sat in the
yellowy light, looking at the white linen and the heavy silver-
ware. Around her neck she still had the green scarab.

I still couldn't believe it, that she was really sitting there:
Sylvia, in person across from me. I looked at her as a
goldminer looks at the priceless nugget he has just dug up
from the riverbed. I hardly knew what we ate and drank; in
my memory that evening can only be compared with the day
of our first meeting – but it was darker, more elusive. She
was pregnant. She had asked if I wanted a child from her, I
had said yes, and she had taken care of it via a ruthless detour

— in a way which until now I had only seen in politics.

'Shall we dance?'

We were in a large, crowded discotheque with walls of polished steel and white, vinyl seats. The crowd was young, mainly Surinam and Indonesian. The dance floor had coloured spotlights flashing on and off and in the thundering sound of the music I wanted to take her small hyroglyphlike body in the white dress into my arms, but she stepped away from me and danced with bare feet in the isolated manner which belonged to the music.

At the bar she drank gin fizz. That was from her time with Alfred. I had to think of him, walking up and down in his room in London. I dreaded the conversation tomorrow morning. I had thought that the afternoon in Hotel Hannie was the last time I would ever sit across from him, but now I would have to go through it again. I felt sorry for him, as he had for me, but at the same time I felt some kind of triumph. He didn't even exist. He had only been used for some kind of artificial insemination.

Sylvia put her head on my shoulder. Every time that I felt her, or when I had looked away and then at her again, there was a sensation of incredulity that she was really here. But the steel fire-screen between me and the facts had not yet been raised. When I searched my purse for my lighter I felt the small bottle with its tablets for blood pressure. Would that suddenly straighten itself out now? No, that would stay this way, like a woman's breasts which after the birth of a child will never be firm again. Or did it mean that I would keep some hidden resentment against her. The kind of thing that comes out when you quarrel about something else, so that any disagreement has the threat of a potential vulcano?

'Yes, how are we going to do this, I wonder?' asked Sylvia.

She had thrown off her dress and was walking around the various rooms in her panties and bra, a glass of beer in her hand. Her hair was tangled. I too had drunk too much. I lay on the sofa exhausted, but not only from drinking.

'What?'

'The babyroom. Where should it be?'

The babyroom. Of course. We had to have one. I stood up to put on another record.

'We can use my study for that.'

'Okay. Then we'll have it papered and painted, and we'll buy a cradle and a commode. But where will you do your work then?'

'There is an attic upstairs.'

'I've never seen it. Let's go and have a look.'

'Do you think we can navigate the stairs?'

The stairs were really more like a ladder, very steep and narrow. I hadn't been up there for years. Because there was no electricity I took a candle. We passed the third floor which belonged to the neighbours and could only be reached by the other front door, and came to the dark, disorderly attic. Everywhere there were the broken wooden walls of rooms in which people had lived in the course of the centuries — some with small windows with or without glass; under our feet the boards crunched with coaldust. Here and there were dust covered suitcases with some of my father's papers, a broken bidet and an old linen closet of my mother's with a mirror in the door. Lopsided on a nail hung a framed reproduction of The Old King by Rouault, which used to hang in Alfred's study above the fireplace. It was warm and stuffy.

'Watch out,' I said.

I pulled the iron bar away from a wooden trapdoor and threw it open. Under the stars lay Amsterdam. We looked at each other — then we embraced and for a little while we stood motionless against each other.

'Wait,' I said, when she wanted to pull me onto the floor.

In my one hand I still had the candle; I put it on the windowsill and opened the linen closet. I pulled out of it a long white piece of cloth, and put it on the floor. After that we made love, but differently from before — much more relaxed and without the sharp tic at the back of the head, because after all there were three of us now. I put my ear against her stomach, she put her hands tenderly on my head and my cheek.

'Can you hear something, father?' she asked.

'Sylvia,' I said, raising myself with a small laugh. 'Have you no fear of anything?'

When at eleven-thirty the next morning Alfred was due to meet Sylvia, I found I couldn't stay at my work any longer. The window of my room at the museum looked out onto a lawn which needed generations to reach its state of perfection. At the end of it was the small eighteenth century teahouse where old Zinnicq Bergmann used to read in the afternoon. I stared at it and asked myself if it was possible that she might let herself be persuaded by him. Perhaps, after a while I would find a note on the table saying that she realized she had been the victim of an illusion and that in the interest of the child she had to go back to Alfred since a woman could never replace a father. But then it seemed to me to be out of the question. Anyone who had so ruthlessly carried out her will could not be easily persuaded. On the other hand I considered her capable of anything. Perhaps she had decided to let go of both of us, to become both the father and mother of the child. Or perhaps the whole affair suddenly sickened her and she would abort the child and disappear out of our lives forever.

With determination I put these thoughts away. I took a piece of paper and wrote:

'Dear mama!

Our life is like a crumpled ball of paper which the cat plays with. One moment it lies in this corner, the next in that, and in the end it seems that we were wrong about that too, and that we did not know ourselves which corner we really were in. The way your life has passed I can only know about from the outside of course, but I believe that all in all it was tranquil and according to the way you planned it. It was of course terrible that papa died so early but you were able to deal with that, with dignity as befits a lady of the old style, and you retain that style in Nice. But just because you are what you are, makes difficulties for me because life has treated me very differently. I was married and divorced, and afterwards met a young woman. I really believed that I did the right thing when lying to you, that time in May but my friend made a mess of it, even though that was not her intention. She could have been your grandaughter, she has no idea what you still represent. I don't represent it either, but at least I still know what it's all about. I know, I don't write very clearly. That's because I'm still in the middle of all kinds of difficult situations, but I believe they will soon be finished. Then no doubt there will be other problems, but somehow I'll be able to handle those too when the time comes.

I won't bother you with it all. I only hope one thing: that this ridiculous tension between us does not continue. I would like you to accept my apologies. Then I'll come right away to Nice, so that. . .'

The phone rang. I thought right away of Sylvia.

'Yes?'

'Is this museum Zinnicq Bergmann?' — a man's voice.

'Yes, who is this?'

'Is Mrs. Tinhuizen there please?'

'Speaking.'

'Mrs. Tinhuizen, this is the police.'

'The. . .'

'There's been an accident.'

'An accident?' I stammered. 'Who is it?' But I already knew.

'With your room-mate. We don't know her name.'

'What's happened to her?'

'She's seriously injured, madam. There's a car on its way to pick you up.'

'What happened!' At that moment I heard the siren of an

approaching police car at the front. 'I'm coming!' I called hoarsely, dropped the receiver on the desk and ran downstairs. Mr. Roebljov sat at the guestbook, he took his glasses off and got up, but I was already outside. A blue light was turning on the roof of the car. An officer held the door open like a cabdriver, got in after me and we drove away. I pulled at his epaulets.

'What happened, what happened?'

'I couldn't tell you madam,' he said quietly removing my hands. 'We only have orders to pick you up. Over the radio. We don't know any more.'

I leaned backward. Of course it couldn't possibly be alright, of course it couldn't possibly be alright, he had kicked and beaten her, thrown her down the stairs, I should have fled with her right away and hidden with our child, gone underground, out of the country. The siren howled; houses, street corners, the whole city raced past, left and right I heard the squealing of braking cars. Other police cars and an ambulance were in front of my house. There was a crowd.

'That's what you get for your dirty business!' called my woman neighbour when I ran to the open door. 'Slut!'

Upstairs it was full of detectives and constables in uniform. 'Where is she?'

'Mrs. . .' said a plain clothes man in the hall and he tried to intercept me.

But I was already in the room. I stopped. I saw right away that she was dead. She lay half on the sofa, half on the floor, like the collapsed Nike of Samothrace. Half of her face had disappeared under the blood, her white dress was torn and red. The sofa, the carpet, the table, the book of Moreau, everything was splattered with blood. One of her hands had disappeared in the tatters and the blood of her stomach. What was left of her face showed her anguish.

A chair was pushed under me.

'Do you know the victim, Mrs. Tinhuizen?'

I nodded.

'Did she live in this house?'

I nodded.

'A love story, it seems to us. She was shot in the head, the heart and the stomach. The shot in the heart was fatal.'

I nodded and looked at the champagne cork which lay on the floor near the window.

'Do you know the suspect? He phoned us himself, but for the rest he only told us where we could reach you. He is in a state of shock.'

With a finger he pointed to my study. I turned my head and saw Alfred: he was pacing rapidly up and down, his mouth hanging open, his arms slack at his sides. On the chair of my desk sat a policeman, his hat on my blotter.

'Alfred Boeken. My ex-husband.'

'Oh. Pardon me. We won't bother you any longer, madam. Only the name of the girl too, please. We have to notify her parents.'

'Sylvia. Sylvia Nithart from Petten.'

'Thank you madam. That's all.'

The old lady in black has told me that I can stay as long as I like. How long do I want to stay? I've been here a week now, I should have buried my mother long ago, but I haven't been in touch with anyone. I watched this afternoon while on the other side of the street my car was picked up by the police and towed away. I didn't do anything about it. I can walk fairly well again, like a circus bear on a ball.

How long do I want to stay? I have nothing else to report. From one dead I travelled to the other. Sylvia lies in her grave in the dunes, our child buried inside her. In Nice lies my mother, embalmed, waiting for me in a cellar. In Amsterdam Alfred sits in a cell; he will have time to spare now and to write his book about the theatre. In the room behind mine the old lady potters about, opposite me is the popes' palace; immediately under my window gapes the hole like a waiting grave.

I can be all the way to the bottom before the echo of my cry comes back.